R Programming for AI

Learn to Build Intelligent Models, Analyze Data, and Unlock AI's Full Potential Using R's Cutting-Edge Tools and Libraries

Peter Simon

2

3

Discover others in the series

**"R Programming for Beginners:
Master the Fundamentals of R, Even with Zero
Coding Experience"**

**"R Programming for Bioinformatics: Analysis of
Genomic and Biological Data"**

**"R Programming for Data Analysis:The Complete
Beginner-to-Expert Guide to Unlocking Insights
from Data"**

**"R Programming for Machine Learning:Building
Predictive Models"**

**"R Programming for Statistical Analysis:Unlock
the Power of Data-Driven Insights"**

Disclaimer

This book, *"R Programming for AI: Learn to Build Intelligent Models, Analyze Data, and Unlock AI's Full Potential Using R's Cutting-Edge Tools and Libraries"*, by **Peter Simon**, is intended for **educational and informational purposes only**.

The content presented in this book is designed to help readers understand and explore the use of the R programming language in the fields of artificial intelligence, machine learning, and data analysis.

Introduction

In the fast-changing world of artificial intelligence (AI), using data well is key. More and more, companies depend on data to make smart choices. This has made experts in data analysis and AI very important.

R is a top programming language for working with data and AI. It's great for statistical computing and showing data in a clear way.

"R Language for AI" is your guide to AI with R. It's perfect for anyone new to AI or looking to grow their skills. This book will help you use R's tools to tackle AI challenges.

In this book, we'll cover the basics of R and how to work with data. You'll learn to build smart models that help make predictions. You'll get both the theory and practical examples to apply AI to real problems.

You will learn how to use R's vast library of tools. This includes `tidyverse` for data work, `caret` for machine learning, and `keras` for deep learning. Each chapter builds on the last, making sure you understand and grow.

By the end, you'll not only know how to use R for AI. You'll also think deeply about AI's potential in your field.

As we start exploring R and AI, get ready for a fascinating journey. You'll learn more than just coding. You'll understand how to interpret results and find insights.

The world of AI is about more than just data and algorithms. It's about telling stories, solving problems, and making a difference.

Let's begin this exciting journey to unlock R's AI potential. Together, we'll turn data into valuable knowledge!

Chapter 1: The Power of R for Artificial Intelligence

In the world of data science and artificial intelligence (AI), picking the right programming language is key. R has become a top choice for data analysis and machine learning. It started as a tool for statistical computing in the mid-1990s.

Now, R is a powerful tool that blends statistics with AI capabilities. It has a wide range of packages and libraries. This makes it great for both simple data analysis and complex model building.

We will explore what makes R stand out for AI. We'll look at its strengths and when it's at its best.

The Statistical Foundation

R was built for statistical analysis. This gives it an advantage in AI, especially in data interpretation and model evaluation. Traditional machine learning focuses on algorithms and speed. But, knowing the statistical basics behind these models can make them better and easier to understand.

Key Statistical Functions

R offers many built-in functions for statistical operations. These are key for AI tasks like regression analysis and data visualization. For example, functions like `lm()` for linear models and `glm()` for generalized linear models help a lot.

These tools make it easy to develop models. They let AI experts test ideas, check hypotheses, and improve their methods with solid statistical analysis.

Comprehensive Libraries for AI

R's biggest plus is its vast library system. CRAN, the Comprehensive R Archive Network, has thousands of packages. Many of these packages are made for AI and machine learning.

Machine Learning Frameworks

Packages like `caret`, `randomForest`, and `xgboost` provide robust frameworks for implementing machine learning algorithms. The `caret` package, for instance, streamlines the process of model training, parameter tuning, and evaluation, enabling data scientists to apply multiple algorithms with ease. It abstracts much of the complexity associated with machine learning into a cohesive workflow, making it accessible even for those who may not be deeply versed in programming.

Deep Learning with R

With the emergence of deep learning, R has not been left behind. The `keras` and `tensorflow` packages allow practitioners to define and train deep learning models natively in R. These tools bridge the gap between the high-level constructs of deep learning and R's analytical strengths, allowing data scientists to leverage the robustness of neural networks while still taking advantage of R's statistical capabilities.

Data Visualization

Effective data visualization serves as a linchpin in both the data exploration phase and the presentation of AI findings to stakeholders. R shines in this domain, providing powerful visualization libraries such as

`ggplot2`, `lattice`, and `plotly`. ### The Art of Visualization in AI

Using these libraries, practitioners can create compelling visual narratives that elucidate complex model outputs, highlight trends, and communicate insights clearly. R's grammar of graphics, established by

`ggplot2`, allows users to understand and apply visualization principles systematically, leading to more thoughtful and less cluttered representations of data.

Community and Collaboration

The R community is vibrant and engaged, characterized by a collaborative spirit that fuels innovation. The open-source nature of R encourages users to contribute, share their packages, and enhance the ecosystem collectively. Platforms like GitHub and R-bloggers further facilitate the flow of ideas and collaboration among practitioners, researchers, and entrepreneurs.

Collaborative Projects

Many academic institutions and industries adopt R for their data science initiatives, resulting in a wealth of shared resources ranging from tutorials to fully developed packages. This collaborative environment can amplify the learning curve for those new to R, enabling a community-driven approach to problem-solving in AI.

Versatility in Applications

R's versatility makes it suitable for a wide range of AI applications, from natural language processing (NLP) to computer vision, and everything in between. Its adaptability allows practitioners to manipulate and analyze data derived from various sources, making it an appealing choice for industries like finance, healthcare, marketing, and social sciences.

R for AI: Benefits, Capabilities, and Ecosystem

In recent years, the demand for data science and artificial intelligence (AI) has surged, propelling programming languages that can efficiently handle data analysis and model building to the forefront. Among these, R has emerged as a powerful tool, especially in academic and research settings. This chapter explores the benefits and capabilities of R in the realm of AI, along with the vibrant ecosystem that supports its use.

The Rise of R in Data Science

R is a language and environment specifically designed for statistical computing and data visualization. It was developed by statisticians for statisticians, allowing analysts and data scientists to perform complex calculations with ease. Its rich set of built-in libraries for data manipulation, statistical analysis, and graphical representation makes it particularly appealing for AI applications.

Benefits of R in AI

Statistical Power: R offers an extensive suite of statistical techniques, from basic linear models to advanced machine learning algorithms. It supports hypothesis testing, regression analysis, time-series analysis, and more, making it invaluable in a data-driven AI environment.

Data Visualization: One of R's greatest strengths lies in its visualization capabilities. Libraries such as ggplot2 enable users to create a variety of static and interactive graphics. Visualization is crucial in AI, as it not only helps in understanding data distributions but also in interpreting the results of complex algorithms.

Community and Support: R has a longstanding, robust community. The Comprehensive R Archive Network (CRAN) hosts thousands of packages contributed by users around the globe, covering various domains. This community ensures that users have access to a wealth of knowledge and resources, making it easier to tackle AI-related challenges.

User-Friendly Interface: RStudio, the most popular integrated development environment (IDE) for R, offers a user-friendly interface that includes syntax highlighting, direct access to help documentation, and an integrated terminal. These features facilitate a smoother workflow for both beginners and experienced data scientists.

Reproducibility: R promotes reproducible research through its strong support for dynamic reporting. Tools like R Markdown allow users to weave together narrative text with code and results, creating documents that can be shared and scrutinized, enhancing transparency in AI development.

Capabilities of R in AI

Machine Learning and Predictive Modeling: R provides access to a multitude of machine learning frameworks such as caret, randomForest, and xgboost. These libraries enable data scientists to implement and compare various algorithms effortlessly, which is vital for developing predictive models.

Text Mining and Natural Language Processing (NLP): With packages like tm and quanteda, R supports text mining and NLP, which are essential in AI fields such as sentiment analysis, topic modeling, and language translation. This capability opens up a range of applications, from chatbots to customer service automation.

Deep Learning: Although traditionally a stronghold of languages like Python, R has made significant strides in deep learning with packages like keras and tensorflow. These libraries allow R users to leverage powerful neural networks for complex AI tasks, such as image and speech recognition.

Time Series Analysis: R is extensively used for time series forecasting, an important aspect of AI in sectors like finance and economics. Packages such as forecast make it easier to analyze temporal data and create forecasts.

Integration with Other Technologies: R's capabilities can be extended by interfacing with other programming languages and environments. Packages like Rcpp allow users to integrate C++ code, enhancing performance for computationally intensive tasks.

The R Ecosystem

The R ecosystem is rich and diverse, comprising not only the R language itself but also an array of packages, tools, and platforms that enhance its AI functionalities.

CRAN and Bioconductor: The Comprehensive R Archive Network (CRAN) offers a repository of packages, while Bioconductor focuses on bioinformatics, providing specialized tools for genomic data analysis. Both platforms play a crucial role in extending R's capabilities for specific fields.

Shiny: Shiny is an R package that facilitates the creation of interactive web applications directly from

R. This integration allows data scientists to build user-friendly interfaces that enable stakeholders to interact with AI models and visualizations without needing to understand the underlying R code.

plumber: The plumber package allows for the easy creation of APIs from R scripts. This capability enables R users to serve their AI models and algorithms as web services, making integration with other applications seamless.

RStudio and Development Tools: Tools such as RMarkdown, Shiny, and the Tidyverse packages provide a cohesive environment for data analysis, modeling, and reporting. This integration streamlines the development process and enhances productivity.

Collaboration with Python and Other Languages: The reticulate package allows R to interface with Python, enabling data scientists to utilize both languages' strengths. This interoperability fosters a multi-disciplinary approach to AI projects, borrowing the best techniques and tools from each language.

R stands out as a potent tool in the AI landscape, thanks to its unique blend of statistical prowess, visualization capabilities, and a supportive ecosystem. Its strengths in data manipulation and analysis, coupled with the rapid development of packages for machine learning and deep learning, position it as a valuable asset for data scientists and AI practitioners. As the fields of data science and AI continue to evolve, R's adaptability, community support, and comprehensive toolkit will ensure its relevance and utility for years to come.

Setting Up Your R Environment for AI Development

This chapter will guide you through setting up your R environment for AI development, including installing necessary packages, configuring your workspace, and ensuring you are prepared to tackle AI projects with proficiency.

1. Installing R and RStudio

Before you dive into AI development with R, you need to install R and an Integrated Development Environment (IDE).

1.1 Installing R

Download R: Go to the Comprehensive R Archive Network (CRAN) at https://cran.r-project.org/.

Choose Your Operating System: Select the appropriate installation file for Windows, macOS, or

Linux.

Follow Installation Instructions: Execute the downloaded file and follow the prompts to install R on your computer.

1.2 Installing RStudio

RStudio is a popular IDE for R, providing a user-friendly interface and essential tools for development.

Download RStudio: Visit https://www.rstudio.com/products/rstudio/download/.

Choose the Free Version: Select the open-source edition compatible with your operating system.

Install RStudio: After downloading, open the installer and follow the instructions to complete the installation.

2. Configuring Your R Environment

Once you have R and RStudio installed, it's time to configure your environment for AI development. ### 2.1 R Packages for AI and Machine Learning

To work effectively on AI projects, you'll need various R packages that facilitate machine learning and data manipulation.

2.1.1 Essential Packages

tidyverse: A suite of packages for data manipulation and visualization.

```R
install.packages("tidyverse")
```

caret: A unified interface for various machine learning algorithms.

```R
install.packages("caret")
```

randomForest: An implementation of the random forest algorithm.

```R
install.packages("randomForest")
```

glmnet: For regularized regression models.

```R
install.packages("glmnet")
```

xgboost: An efficient and scalable implementation of gradient boosting.

```R
install.packages("xgboost")
```

keras: An R interface to the Keras library, which is useful for deep learning.

```R
install.packages("keras")
```

tidymodels: A framework for modeling in a tidy way.

```R
install.packages("tidymodels")
```

2.1.2 Installing Packages

You can install R packages using the console in RStudio:

```R
install.packages(c("tidyverse", "caret", "randomForest", "glmnet", "xgboost", "keras", "tidymodels"))
```

Once installed, you can load the packages in your script using the library function:

```R
library(tidyverse)           library(caret)
library(randomForest) library(glmnet) library(xgboost)
library(keras) library(tidymodels)
```

2.2 Setting Your R Project

Creating R projects in RStudio helps in organizing your files and scripts.

Create a New Project: Click on 'File' > 'New Project'.

Choose Project Type: Select a directory to store your project files.

Naming: Give your project an appropriate name related to your AI development work.

Organize Your Workspace: Populate your project directory with subfolders for data, scripts, and results.

2.3 Version Control with Git

Implementing version control in your AI projects allows for better collaboration and tracking of changes.

Install Git: Visit https://git-scm.com/ and download the installer for your operating

19

system.

Integrate Git with RStudio: Within RStudio, navigate to `Tools` > `Global Options` > `Git/SVN` and set your Git executable path.

Initialize Git Repository: In your project, create a new Git repository via the terminal or using RStudio's Git pane.

3. Data Sources for AI Development

An essential part of AI development is having access to relevant datasets. Here are resources to find datasets suitable for your projects:

Kaggle: A popular platform for data science competitions where you can download datasets.

UCI Machine Learning Repository: A collection of databases for empirical studies of machine learning algorithms.

Open Data Portals: Websites like Data.gov provide open access to data collected by government agencies.

4. Learning Resources

To deepen your understanding of AI development in R, consider the following resources:

Books: Titles like "R for Data Science" by Hadley Wickham and "Hands-On Machine Learning with R" by Bruno Granholi.

Online Courses: Websites like Coursera and edX offer numerous courses on R programming and machine learning.

Forums: Engage with communities on platforms like

Stack Overflow or the RStudio Community forum for questions and support.

Setting up your R environment for AI development is the crucial first step to entering the field of data science and AI. By installing R and RStudio, configuring your environment with essential packages, effectively organizing your workspace, and utilizing version control, you place yourself in a robust position to embark on your AI journey. With the right tools and resources, you can develop sophisticated models, analyze complex datasets, and contribute to the evolving landscape of artificial intelligence.

Chapter 2: Fundamentals of R Programming for AI

This chapter delves into the fundamentals of R programming, particularly focusing on its application in AI, machine learning, and data analysis.

2.1 Introduction to R

R is an open-source programming language and software environment primarily used for statistical computing and graphics. Developed in the early 1990s, it has grown immensely popular among statisticians, data analysts, and AI practitioners due to its flexibility and rich ecosystem of packages.

2.1.1 Installation and Setup

To get started with R, you need to install it alongside RStudio, a powerful IDE that enhances the user experience. Follow these steps:

Download R: Go to [CRAN (Comprehensive R Archive Network)](https://cran.r-project.org/) and choose the appropriate version for your operating system (Windows, macOS, or Linux).

Install R: Run the downloaded installation file and follow the on-screen instructions.

Download RStudio: Next, download RStudio from the [RStudio website](https://www.rstudio.com/products/rstudio/download/) and install it.

Launch RStudio: Once R and RStudio are installed, launch RStudio to start coding in R. ### 2.1.2 Getting

Familiar with RStudio

RStudio provides an integrated workspace that includes four main panels:

Source: Here, you can write and save your R scripts.

Console: Directly interact with R by entering commands and getting immediate feedback.

Environment/History: This panel shows the variables in your workspace and command history for easy navigation.

Files/Plots/Packages/Help: This multifunctional panel allows you to manage files, view plots, install and load packages, and get help.

2.2 Basic R Syntax

Understanding the basic syntax of R is crucial for effective coding. Here are some core concepts: ### 2.2.1 Data Types

R supports several data types:

- **Numeric**: Real numbers (e.g., `1.23`, `4.56`).

Integer: Whole numbers (e.g., `1L`, `2L`).

Character: Strings of text (e.g., `"Hello, AI!"`).

Logical: Boolean values (`TRUE`, `FALSE`).

2.2.2 Data Structures

Common data structures include:

Vectors: One-dimensional array-like objects, which can hold elements of the same type.

```R
```

```R
vec <- c(1, 2, 3, 4, 5)
```

Matrices: Two-dimensional, homogeneous data structures.

```R
mat <- matrix(1:6, nrow=2)
```

Data Frames: Two-dimensional, heterogeneous data tables.

```R
df <- data.frame(Name=c("AI", "ML"), Year=c(2021, 2022))
```

Lists: Collections of objects that can be of different types.

```R
lst <- list(Name="R", Version=4.0, Released=2020)
```

2.2.3 Control Structures

Control structures facilitate decision-making and iteration:

Conditional Statements:

```R
if (x > 0) { print("Positive")
```

24

```
} else {
print("Non-positive")
}
```

Loops:

```R
for (i in 1:5) { print(i)
}
```

2.3 Leveraging R for AI

R is particularly beneficial in AI for tasks involving data manipulation, statistical analysis, and visualization. The following sections highlight essential R packages and concepts that empower working with AI.

2.3.1 Key R Packages for AI

Several packages enhance R's capabilities in AI:

caret: A unified interface for creating prediction models.

randomForest: For implementing the random forest algorithm, popular in classification tasks.

gbm: Implement Gradient Boosting Machines for effective predictive modeling.

nnet: Build neural network models allowing complex learning capabilities.

tidyverse: A collection of packages that simplify data manipulation and visualization. ### 2.3.2 Data

25

Preprocessing

Before applying algorithms, data preprocessing is vital to ensure quality and relevance:

Data Cleaning: Handle missing values and outliers.

```R
df <- na.omit(df)
```

Normalization: Scale data for improved algorithm performance.

```R
df$scaled_column <- scale(df$original_column)
```

Feature Engineering: Create new features that enhance model performance. ### 2.3.3 Model Training and Evaluation

Training AI models in R involves several steps:

Splitting Data: Divide datasets into training and testing sets.

```R set.seed(123)
train_index <- sample(1:nrow(df), 0.8 * nrow(df))
train_data <- df[train_index, ]

test_data <- df[-train_index, ]
```

Fitting Models: Use suitable algorithms for model

training.

```R
model <- train(target ~ ., data=train_data, method='rf')
```

Evaluating Model Performance: Use metrics such as accuracy, confusion matrix, or ROC curves.

```R
predictions <- predict(model, test_data)
confusionMatrix(predictions, test_data$target)
```

We explored the fundamentals of R programming, emphasizing its significance in AI. From basic syntax and data structures to advanced AI applications, R provides a solid framework for tackling data-driven challenges. Mastering R will not only enhance your AI capabilities but also empower you to make data- informed decisions in your projects.

Essential R Syntax, Data Types, and Control Structures

R is a versatile programming language predominantly used for statistical analysis, data visualization, and data science. Understanding its syntax, data types, and control structures is essential for effectively leveraging R's capabilities. This chapter will walk you through the foundational aspects of R, providing you with the essential tools for writing efficient and effective code.

R Syntax

1. Basic Syntax

In R, expressions are typically written in a straightforward manner. Comments in R begin with the `#` symbol and are ignored during execution. For example:

```r

# This is a comment in R

print("Hello, World!")  # This prints a message to the console

```

2. Functions and Assignment

Functions are a fundamental part of R. To create a function, you use the `function` keyword. An assignment is typically performed using the `<-` operator, although `=` can also be used.

```r

# Assigning a value to a variable x <- 10

# Defining a function my_function <- function(y) {

result <- y + x  # Accessing the variable x return(result)

}

# Calling the function my_function(5) # Returns 15

```

3. Vectors

Vectors are one of the core data structures in R. They can store multiple values of the same type. You create a vector using the `c()` function:

```r
# Creating a numeric vector my_vector <- c(1, 2, 3, 4, 5)
# Accessing elements
my_vector[2]  # Returns the second element, which is 2

```

Data Types

R has several data types, including:

1. Numeric

Numeric values are the default data type for numbers in R. For example:

```r
num <- 10.5  # Numeric type
```

2. Integer

To explicitly create integer values, append an `L` to the number:

```r
int_value <- 5L # Integer type
```

3. Character

Character data types are used to represent text strings, defined using either single or double quotes:

```r
```

```r
char_value <- "Hello, R!"  # Character type
```

4. Logical

Logical data types can hold `TRUE`, `FALSE`, or `NA` (not available):

```r
is_true <- TRUE  # Logical type
```

5. Factors

Factors are used for categorical data. They can have a fixed number of unique values, known as levels:

```r
categories <- factor(c("Male", "Female", "Female", "Male"))
```

6. Data Frames

Data frames are tabular data structures, similar to spreadsheets, allowing you to store data in rows and columns. Each column can hold different types of data:

```r
# Creating a data frame my_data <- data.frame(
Name = c("John", "Mary", "Paul"),
Age = c(25, 30, 22),
Gender = factor(c("Male", "Female", "Male"))
)
```

```
```

Control Structures

Control structures regulate the flow of execution within your code. The three primary types in R are conditionals, loops, and functions.

1. Conditional Statements

Conditional statements execute code based on whether a specified condition is met. The most common ones are `if`, `else if`, and `else`:

```r
number <- 15

if (number > 10) {

print("Number is greater than 10")

} else if (number == 10) { print("Number is equal to 10")

} else {

print("Number is less than 10")

}
```

2. Loops

Loops allow you to execute a block of code multiple times. The two most common types in R are `for` loops and `while` loops.

For Loop

A `for` loop iterates over a sequence:

```r
```

31

```r
for (i in 1:5) { print(i)
}
```

While Loop

A `while` loop continues executing as long as the condition remains true:

```r
count <- 1
while (count <= 5) { print(count)
count <- count + 1
}
```

3. Using Apply Functions

R provides several `apply` functions, such as `lapply`, `sapply`, and `tapply`, which allow you to apply functions to elements of a list or vectors without the need for explicit loops.

```r
# Using lapply to square elements of a vector
squared_values <- lapply(c(1, 2, 3, 4), function(x) x^2)
```

This chapter provides a foundation from which you can explore more complex topics in R. Keep practicing and experimenting with different data structures and control mechanisms, and you will quickly become more adept at solving data-related problems using R.

Working with Data Frames, Lists, and Tidyverse Tools

This chapter will guide you through the essentials of working with data frames, lists, and the powerful Tidyverse suite of packages in R. Mastery of these components will empower you to preprocess data effectively, build AI models, and derive insights that can lead to better decision-making.

1. Understanding Data Frames in R ### 1.1 What is a Data Frame?

A data frame can be thought of as a table or a spreadsheet where each column represents a variable and each row represents an observation. In R, data frames are one of the most commonly used data structures for performing data analysis.

```r
# Creating a simple data frame data <- data.frame(
Name = c("Alice","Bob","Cathy"), Age = c(25, 30, 22),
Score = c(85.5, 90.0, 88.5)
)
print(data)
```

1.2 Manipulating Data Frames

Data frames come with a variety of built-in functions for manipulation. The base R functions such as

`subset()`, `merge()`, and `aggregate()` enable basic

operations, but Tidyverse tools make these tasks more intuitive and cleaner.

Example: Filtering and Selecting Data

```r
```r library(dplyr)
```

Filtering and selecting columns filtered_data <- data %>% filter(Age > 24) %>% select(Name, Score)

print(filtered_data)
```
```

2. Harnessing Lists in R ### 2.1 What is a List?

A list in R is a versatile data structure that can hold elements of different types, including vectors, data frames, and even other lists. Lists are particularly useful for storing complex data structures and are commonly used in functions that return multiple outputs.

```r
```r
```

Creating a list my_list <- list(DataFrame = data,

Description = "A list containing a data frame and description", Summary = summary(data)

)

print(my_list)
```
```

2.2 Working with Lists

You can access elements in a list using the `$` operator or double square brackets `[[]]`. Lists are invaluable for managing outputs from functions that yield multiple results, especially when preparing data for AI models.

34

```r

# Accessing elements of a list print(my_list$DataFrame)
print(my_list[[3]]) # Accessing the Summary
```

3. Introduction to Tidyverse

The Tidyverse is an ecosystem of R packages designed for data science that promotes a consistent philosophy and syntax, making data manipulation, visualization, and modeling straightforward.

3.1 Key Packages in Tidyverse

ggplot2: For creating elegant data visualizations.

tidyr: For tidying and reshaping data.

dplyr: For data manipulation tasks like filtering and summarizing.

purrr: For functional programming and working with lists. ### 3.2 Basic Tidyverse Functions

Example: Tidying Data with tidyr

```r library(tidyr)

# Converting wide data to long data format wide_data <- data.frame(

Name = c("Alice", "Bob", "Cathy"), Math = c(85, 90, 88),

Science = c(88, 92, 84)

)

long_data <- pivot_longer(wide_data, cols = c(Math, Science), names_to = "Subject", values_to = "Score")
print(long_data)
```

```
```

3.3 Data Visualization with ggplot2

Visualization is key in understanding patterns and deriving insights from data. With `ggplot2`, creating sophisticated graphics is intuitive.

```r
library(ggplot2)

# Basic scatter plot
ggplot(data, aes(x = Age, y = Score)) + geom_point() +
labs(title = "Score vs Age", x = "Age", y = "Score")
```

4. Putting It All Together: A Use Case

Let's consider a use case where we have data on various individuals' ages, scores, and we want to predict future performance using a simple linear regression model.

4.1 Data Preparation First, we will prepare our data:

```r
library(dplyr)

# Simulating some additional data set.seed(42)
data <- data.frame( Name = letters[1:100],
Age = sample(18:60, 100, replace = TRUE), Score =
rnorm(100, mean=75, sd=10)
)

# Data cleaning and selection cleaned_data <- data %>%
filter(!is.na(Age), !is.na(Score)) %>% select(Age, Score)
```

4.2 Building a Model

36

We can build a simple linear regression model using `lm()`:

```r
model <- lm(Score ~ Age, data = cleaned_data)
summary(model)
```

4.3 Making Predictions

Using the model, we can predict scores based on new age data:

```r
new_data <- data.frame(Age = c(20, 30, 40, 50))
predictions <- predict(model, newdata = new_data)
print(predictions)
```

We explored the fundamental components of data manipulation in R using data frames and lists and how the Tidyverse enhances these processes. By familiarizing yourself with these tools, you are now equipped to handle data more effectively, a vital skill in the world of artificial intelligence. As you continue your journey in data science, remember that the capabilities of R, especially through the lens of Tidyverse, offer a flexible and powerful foundation for your AI projects. End of the chapter.

Chapter 3: Data Preprocessing and Exploration

This chapter delves into the crucial steps of data preprocessing and exploration using R, a versatile and powerful language for statistical analysis and data visualization.

3.1 Introduction to Data Preprocessing

Data preprocessing is the initial step in the data analysis pipeline that involves transforming raw data into a clean dataset suitable for analysis. It encompasses a broad range of activities such as data cleaning, normalization, transformation, and encoding categorical variables. For any AI application, preprocessing is a critical step to ensure that the models trained on the data yield reliable predictions.

3.1.1 Importance of Data Quality

Before delving into preprocessing techniques, it's important to understand why data quality matters. Poor quality data can lead to incorrect predictions, biased outcomes, and, ultimately, failed AI projects. Therefore, investing time and effort in data preprocessing is fundamental to the overall success of any AI initiative.

3.2 Importing Data in R

R offers a wealth of packages that facilitate the import of various data formats such as CSV, Excel, JSON, and databases. The `readr` and `readxl` packages are popular choices for data import.

```R
```

```
# Importing a CSV file using readr library(readr)
data <- read_csv("path/to/your/datafile.csv")
# Importing an Excel file using readxl library(readxl)
data <- read_excel("path/to/your/datafile.xlsx")
```

Once the data is imported, it is essential to take a preliminary look at it to understand its structure and contents.

3.3 Exploratory Data Analysis (EDA)

EDAs are imperative for gaining insights into the dataset. This phase allows data scientists to visualize distributions, identify patterns, and recognize anomalies.

3.3.1 Summary Statistics

The first step in EDA is obtaining summary statistics. The `summary()` function in R provides a quick overview of numerical variables.

```R
summary(data)
```

3.3.2 Data Visualization

Visualization is a powerful tool in data exploration. R has extensive capabilities for visualization, with popular packages such as `ggplot2`. Here are some examples of visualizations you can create:

Histograms for Distribution

```R
library(ggplot2)
ggplot(data,      aes(x=your_numeric_variable))      +
```

```
geom_histogram(binwidth=1, fill="blue", color="black")
+ labs(title="Histogram of Your Variable", x="Value",
y="Frequency")
```

Boxplots for Outlier Detection

Boxplots are effective for identifying outliers and understanding the spread of data.

```R
ggplot(data, aes(x=factor(your_categorical_variable),
y=your_numeric_variable)) + geom_boxplot() +

labs(title="Boxplot of Your Variable by Category",
x="Category", y="Value")
```

Correlation Matrix Heatmap

Understanding correlations between variables can help in feature selection.

```R
library(reshape2)

correlation_matrix <- cor(data[numeric_columns]) #
Adjust for your numeric columns melted_correlation <-
melt(correlation_matrix)

ggplot(data = melted_correlation, aes(Var1, Var2,
fill=value)) + geom_tile() +

scale_fill_gradient2(low="blue",          high="red",
mid="white",          limit=c(-1,1),          space="Lab",
name="Correlation") +

theme_minimal()   +   labs(title="Correlation   Matrix
Heatmap")
```

```
```

3.4 Data Cleaning

3.4.1 Handling Missing Values

Missing values are commonplace in real-world datasets, and how you handle them can significantly affect model performance. You can choose to remove or impute them.

```R
# Remove rows with any missing values clean_data <- na.omit(data)

# Alternatively, impute missing values (e.g., mean imputation)
data$your_numeric_variable[is.na(data$your_numeric_variable)] <- mean(data$your_numeric_variable, na.rm = TRUE)
```

3.4.2 Addressing Outliers

Outliers can skew results and should be addressed carefully. You can identify outliers using various methods such as the IQR rule or Z-scores.

```R
# Using the IQR method

Q1 <- quantile(data$your_numeric_variable, 0.25) Q3 <- quantile(data$your_numeric_variable, 0.75)

IQR <- Q3 - Q1

outlier_threshold_upper <- Q3 + 1.5 * IQR outlier_threshold_lower <- Q1 - 1.5 * IQR
```

41

```
# Remove outliers
clean_data    <-    data[data$your_numeric_variable    <
outlier_threshold_upper & data$your_numeric_variable
> outlier_threshold_lower, ]
```

3.5 Feature Engineering

Feature engineering is the process of creating new features that can improve model performance. This includes encoding categorical variables, creating interaction terms, or deriving new features from existing data.

3.5.1 Encoding Categorical Variables

Machine learning algorithms require numerical input, so it is crucial to convert categorical variables into a suitable format using techniques like one-hot encoding.

```R
# One-hot encoding with dplyr and tidyr library(dplyr)
library(tidyr)
data_encoded <- data %>%
mutate(your_categorical_variable                         =
as.factor(your_categorical_variable)) %>%
pivot_wider(names_from = your_categorical_variable,
values_from = your_numeric_variable, values_fill = 0)
```

3.5.2 Normalization and Scaling

Normalizing features is essential when variables have

different units or scales. The `scale()` function can standardize your data.

```R

data_scaled <- scale(data[numeric_columns]) # Select numeric columns only

```

Data preprocessing and exploration are vital steps in the machine learning pipeline. This chapter has provided an overview of how to perform these tasks in R effectively. By ensuring high data quality through thorough cleaning and exploration techniques, you set the foundation for building robust AI models. The next chapter will delve into choosing the right AI algorithms and implementing them with the preprocessed data.

Data Cleaning, Transformation, and Feature Engineering

The process of preparing data—commonly referred to as data cleaning, transformation, and feature engineering—is a crucial step in the data science pipeline. In this chapter, we will explore these concepts in the context of R, a versatile programming language that is widely used for statistical analysis and data visualization.

1. Introduction to Data Cleaning

Data cleaning, also known as data scrubbing, involves identifying and correcting inaccuracies or inconsistencies in your dataset. It is an essential step because even small errors can lead to misleading analysis results and poor predictions. Common tasks in data cleaning include:

43

Handling Missing Values: Missing data is ubiquitous in real-world datasets. In R, we can identify missing values using functions like `is.na()`, and we have several strategies to manage them:

Deletion: Removing rows or columns that contain missing values (using `na.omit()`).

Imputation: Filling in missing values using various techniques, such as mean, median, or mode substitution (using the `imputeTS` package).

```R
library(imputeTS)

data$column_with_nas <- na_mean(data$column_with_nas) # Mean imputation
```

Correcting Data Types: Ensuring that each variable is of the correct type (e.g., integer, factor, character). This can be done using `as.numeric()`, `as.character()`, and `as.factor()` functions.

```R
data$column_as_factor <- as.factor(data$column_as_factor)
```

Identifying Outliers: Outliers can skew your analysis. R provides various methods for detection, such as visual inspection using boxplots:

```R
boxplot(data$column)
```

44

You can also use statistical methods like Z-scores or the IQR method for identifying outliers. ## 2. Data Transformation

Data transformation refers to the process of converting data into a format that is more suitable for analysis. It often involves normalizing, scaling, or encoding features to improve model performance.

Normalization and Scaling: Scaling features ensures that they contribute equally to the distance calculations in algorithms, especially in k-nearest neighbors (KNN) and gradient descent. Normalization scales data to a range between [0,1], while standardization scales it to have a mean of 0 and a standard deviation of 1.

```R
# Scaling data using Min-Max normalization

data$scaled_column       <-       (data$column       -
min(data$column))       /       (max(data$column)       -
min(data$column))


# Z-score    normalization    data$scaled_column    <-
scale(data$column)
```

Encoding Categorical Variables: Many machine learning algorithms require numerical inputs, so categorical variables must be encoded. The most common methods are one-hot encoding and label encoding.

```R
```

```
# One-hot encoding with the `dplyr` and `tidyr` packages
library(dplyr)
library(tidyr)

data <- data %>%
mutate(category = as.factor(category)) %>%
pivot_wider(names_from = category, values_from = category, values_fill = 0, values_fn = length)
```

Date and Time Manipulation: Working with datetime variables is crucial in many data science tasks. R provides the `lubridate` package to simplify datetime manipulations.

```R
library(lubridate)
data$date_column <- ymd(data$date_column) # Parse date
```

3. Feature Engineering

Feature engineering is the process of creating new features from existing data to improve model performance. It often requires creativity and domain knowledge.

Creating Interaction Terms: Sometimes, the interaction between features can capture more complex relationships. You can create new features that are products or combinations of existing features.

```R
```

```
data$interaction_feature     <-     data$feature1     *
data$feature2
```

Binning: Converting numerical variables into categorical bins can enhance the model's ability to capture non-linear relationships.

```R
data$age_group <- cut(data$age, breaks=c(0, 18, 35, 50, 100), labels=c("0-18", "19-35", "36-50", "51+"))
```

Polynomial Features: For linear models, you can create polynomial features to handle non-linear relationships between the predictor and target variables.

```R
data$feature1_squared <- data$feature1^2
```

Target Encoding: For categorical features, target encoding involves replacing categories with a statistic (like mean or median) of the target variable.

```R
library(encode)
data$encoded_category     <-     encode(data$category, data$target_variable, method = "mean")
```

4. Bringing It All Together

The process of data cleaning, transformation, and feature engineering is iterative and may require multiple cycles of refinement. Each step is highly contextual, depending on the specific dataset and the machine learning model being used. It is important to document all transformations applied to the data for reproducibility and validation purposes.

In R, leveraging packages such as `dplyr`, `tidyr`, and `lubridate`, along with visualization libraries like

`ggplot2`, can enhance these processes significantly. Furthermore, using workflows that incorporate good coding practices can help maintain the quality and clarity of your data preparation process.

Data cleaning, transformation, and feature engineering are critical components of preparing data for AI and ML projects. They directly influence the accuracy and effectiveness of predictive models. By mastering these techniques in R, you equip yourself with powerful tools to enhance your data-driven decision-making capabilities in AI realms.

Exploratory Data Analysis (EDA) with ggplot2 and dplyr

Exploratory Data Analysis (EDA) is a crucial step in the data analysis process. It allows researchers and data scientists to summarize the main characteristics of the dataset, often using visual methods. By understanding the underlying patterns and relationships in the data, one can make informed decisions about which analytical methods to employ in subsequent stages. In this chapter, we will explore how to effectively utilize the `ggplot2` and `dplyr` packages in R to conduct EDA, uncover insights, and visually represent findings.

Setting Up the Environment

Before diving into EDA, you need to ensure your R environment is set up with the necessary packages. Start by installing and loading the required libraries:

```R
install.packages(c("ggplot2", "dplyr")) library(ggplot2)
library(dplyr)
```

We will work with a sample dataset, commonly used in EDA practices – the `mtcars` dataset, which contains various specifications and performance measurements of different car models.

```R
data(mtcars) head(mtcars)
```

Data Wrangling with dplyr

The first step in EDA is often preparing and cleaning the data. The `dplyr` package offers an intuitive set of functions for data manipulation, allowing us to filter, arrange, summarize, and mutate data easily.

Filtering Data

To focus on a specific subset of data, we can use the `filter()` function. For example, let's filter the dataset to include cars with more than 20 miles per gallon (mpg):

```R
high_mpg_cars <- mtcars %>% filter(mpg > 20)
```

```
```

Summarizing Data

The `summarize()` function can aggregate data based on groups. For instance, if we want to find the average horsepower (`hp`) for each number of cylinders (`cyl`), we can do so as follows:

```R
average_hp <- mtcars %>%

group_by(cyl) %>%

summarize(avg_hp = mean(hp, na.rm = TRUE))
```

Creating New Variables

Sometimes, creating new variables can be helpful for analysis. You can achieve this with the `mutate()` function. For example, let's create a new variable that represents the weight of the cars in thousands of pounds:

```R
mtcars <- mtcars %>%

mutate(weight_1000lbs = wt * 2.20462 / 1000)
```

Visualization with ggplot2

Once the data is prepped, the next step is to visualize the data. The `ggplot2` package enables the creation of elaborate and informative graphics with ease.

Scatter Plots

A scatter plot can be useful for examining the relationship

between two continuous variables. For example, to visualize the relationship between horsepower and miles per gallon:

```R
ggplot(mtcars, aes(x = hp, y = mpg)) + geom_point() +

ggtitle("Horsepower vs. Miles Per Gallon") + xlab("Horsepower") +

ylab("Miles Per Gallon")
```

Box Plots

Box plots are excellent for visualizing the distribution of data across different categories. Let's create a box plot to compare the `mpg` across different `cyl` groups.

```R
ggplot(mtcars, aes(x = factor(cyl), y = mpg)) + geom_boxplot() +

ggtitle("Box Plot of MPG by Cylinder Count") + xlab("Number of Cylinders") +

ylab("Miles Per Gallon")
```

Histograms

To understand the distribution of a single variable, histograms are particularly effective. Let's create a histogram to display the distribution of the `mpg` variable.

```R
```

```R
ggplot(mtcars, aes(x = mpg)) +

geom_histogram(bins = 10, fill = "blue", color = "white") +


ggtitle("Histogram of Miles Per Gallon") + xlab("Miles Per Gallon") + ylab("Frequency")
```

Faceting

Faceting allows us to create multiple plots based on a factor variable. For example, let's create a series of scatter plots of `hp` versus `mpg`, faceting by the number of cylinders:

```R
ggplot(mtcars, aes(x = hp, y = mpg)) + geom_point() +

facet_wrap(~cyl) +

ggtitle("Scatter Plot of Horsepower vs. MPG by Cylinder Count") + xlab("Horsepower") +

ylab("Miles Per Gallon")
```

We have covered the essential tools for conducting Exploratory Data Analysis (EDA) in R using the `dplyr` and `ggplot2` packages. By integrating data manipulation with visual exploration, we can effectively uncover insights from our data, laying a solid foundation for subsequent statistical analysis.

Chapter 4: Introduction to Machine Learning in R

Unlike traditional programming, where explicit instructions are coded into a system, machine learning systems are designed to identify patterns and relationships within datasets and then utilize this understanding to inform new insights or automate processes.

This chapter focuses on the implementation of machine learning algorithms using R, a powerful programming environment specifically tailored for data analysis and statistics. R's extensive libraries and user-friendly syntax make it a popular choice among statisticians and data scientists. By leveraging R's capabilities, we can develop models that can predict future outcomes, classify data, and identify trends.

4.2 Getting Started with R

Before diving into machine learning, it's essential to have a solid understanding of R and its ecosystem. The following steps outline how to get started:

4.2.1 Installation

To begin, you need to install R and RStudio, an integrated development environment (IDE) that provides a user-friendly interface for coding in R. Follow these steps:

Download R: Visit the Comprehensive R Archive Network (CRAN) [here](https://cran.r-project.org/) and choose the appropriate version for your operating system (Windows, Mac, or Linux).

Install RStudio: Go to [RStudio's website](https://www.rstudio.com/products/rstudio/download/) and download the RStudio IDE.

4.2.2 Setup

Once R and RStudio are installed, open RStudio. You can create a new script by navigating to File > New File > R Script. This is where you will write and execute your R code.

4.2.3 Required Libraries

Several libraries are essential for machine learning in R. You can install them using the following commands:

```R
install.packages("caret")   # General machine learning
install.packages("randomForest")  # Random Forest
algorithm install.packages("ggplot2")          #
Data visualization install.packages("dplyr")          #
Data manipulation install.packages("e1071")
        # Support vector machine
```

Load the libraries in your R script using:

```R
library(caret)
library(randomForest) library(ggplot2)
library(dplyr) library(e1071)
```

4.3 Understanding Data

Machine learning starts with data, and understanding your dataset is crucial. Data can be categorized into two types: structured (such as tables and spreadsheets) and unstructured (such as text and images).

4.3.1 Data Preparation

Before applying machine learning algorithms, the data needs to be preprocessed. Common preprocessing steps include:

Handling Missing Values: Use techniques like imputation or removal to manage missing values in your dataset.

Normalization and Scaling: Standardize your data to bring all features onto a common scale, especially important for algorithms sensitive to data ranges, such as k-nearest neighbors.

Encoding Categorical Variables: Convert categorical variables into numerical formats using techniques like one-hot encoding.

4.3.2 Exploring the Dataset

Use R's `summary()`, `str()`, and `head()` functions to explore the dataset. Visualizations through `ggplot2` can help uncover patterns and relationships.

```R
# Example of data exploration

data <- read.csv("data.csv")          # Load your dataset summary(data)     # Overview of all variables

ggplot(data, aes(x = feature1, y = feature2)) + geom_point() # Scatter plot
```

```
```

4.4 Choosing an Algorithm

The choice of algorithm depends on your specific task, such as classification, regression, or clustering. Here, we review two popular algorithms:

4.4.1 Decision Trees

Decision trees are intuitive and powerful for both classification and regression tasks. You can implement decision trees using the `rpart` package as follows:

```R
library(rpart)

model <- rpart(target ~ ., data = training_data)
```

4.4.2 Random Forests

Random forests improve upon decision trees by creating an ensemble of trees, which reduces overfitting and improves accuracy. You can train a random forest model using:

```R
model_rf <- randomForest(target ~ ., data = training_data, ntree = 500)
```

4.5 Model Evaluation

Evaluating the performance of your machine learning model is crucial to ensure its reliability. Common metrics include accuracy, precision, recall, and F1-score for classification tasks and RMSE (Root Mean Squared Error) for regression.

Use the `caret` package to split your data into training and testing sets, then apply your trained model to the test data and assess its performance:

```R
R set.seed(123)

train_index <- createDataPartition(data$target, p = 0.8, list = FALSE) train_data <- data[train_index, ]

test_data <- data[-train_index, ]

predictions <- predict(model_rf, test_data)

confusionMatrix(factor(predictions), factor(test_data$target))    # Confusion matrix for classification
```

We introduced the fundamentals of machine learning using R. We covered installation and setup, data exploration, algorithm selection, and model evaluation. With the foundational knowledge of machine learning concepts and the tools available in R, you're now prepared to dive deeper into specific machine learning techniques and their applications.

Supervised Learning: Regression and Classification Basics

This chapter will introduce two fundamental types of supervised learning problems: regression and classification.

1.1 Understanding Regression

Regression is a type of supervised learning task that aims to predict a continuous numeric value based on input features. For instance, predicting housing prices based on various features such as size, location, and number of bedrooms is a regression problem.

1.1.1 Linear Regression

The simplest form of regression is linear regression, which models the relationship between the dependent variable (output) and one or more independent variables (inputs) as a linear equation. The basic formula for a linear relationship can be expressed as:

$$ Y = \beta_0 + \beta_1X_1 + \beta_2X_2 + \ldots + \beta_nX_n + \epsilon $$ Where:

(Y) is the dependent variable

(β_0) is the intercept

$(\beta_1, \beta_2, \ldots, \beta_n)$ are the coefficients of the independent variables

$(X_1, X_2, \ldots, X_n)$ are the independent variables

(ϵ) is the error term

In R, we can implement linear regression using the `lm()` function. Here's a simple example:

```R
# Load necessary libraries library(ggplot2)

# Create a simple dataset data <- data.frame(

size = c(1500, 2000, 2500, 3000, 3500),

price = c(300000, 400000, 500000, 600000, 700000)
```

```
)
# Fit a linear model
model <- lm(price ~ size, data = data)
# Display model summary summary(model)
# Visualize the results
ggplot(data, aes(x = size, y = price)) + geom_point() +
geom_smooth(method = "lm", se = FALSE) +
labs(title = "Housing Price Prediction", x = "Size (sq ft)", y
= "Price ($)")
```

```
```

This script creates a dataset of house sizes and prices, fits a linear model, and visualizes the relationship. ### 1.1.2 Multiple Linear Regression

When multiple independent variables are involved, we use multiple linear regression. This extends the linear model to accommodate more features, enhancing our predictive capability. The fitting process in R follows the same approach as simple linear regression:

```R
# Create a dataset with multiple features data_multiple <-
data.frame(

size = c(1500, 2000, 2500, 3000, 3500),

bedrooms = c(3, 4, 4, 5, 5),

price = c(300000, 400000, 500000, 600000, 700000)
)
```

```
# Fit a multiple linear model

model_multiple <- lm(price ~ size + bedrooms, data =
data_multiple)

# Display model summary summary(model_multiple)
```

In this example, we add the number of bedrooms as
another predictor, allowing the model to provide a more
nuanced prediction of housing prices.

1.2 Understanding Classification

Classification is another type of supervised learning task
where the goal is to predict a categorical label for input
data. A classic example is determining whether an email is
"spam" or "not spam" based on various features of the
email.

1.2.1 Logistic Regression

Despite the name, logistic regression is used for binary
classification rather than regression. It models the
probability that a given input belongs to a particular class
using the logistic function, transforming the output to a
value between 0 and 1. The formula for logistic regression
is:

$$ P(Y=1|X) = \frac{1}{1 + e^{-(\beta_0 + \beta_1 X_1 + ... + \beta_n X_n)}} $$

In R, we implement logistic regression using the `glm()`
function with the family set to "binomial". Here's an
example using a simple dataset:

```R
# Create a simple dataset for classification data_class <-
```

```
data.frame(
hours_studied = c(1, 2, 3, 4, 5),
passed_exam = c(0, 0, 1, 1, 1)
)
# Fit a logistic regression model
model_class <- glm(passed_exam ~ hours_studied,
family = "binomial", data = data_class)


# Display model summary summary(model_class)
# Make predictions
predictions <- predict(model_class, type = "response")
# Create a plot to visualize the results
ggplot(data_class, aes(x = hours_studied, y =
passed_exam)) + geom_point() +
geom_smooth(method = "glm", method.args = list(family
= "binomial"), se = FALSE) + labs(title = "Exam Passing
Probability", x = "Hours Studied", y = "Probability of
Passing")
```
```

In this example, we predict whether the students pass the exam based on the number of hours studied. ### 1.2.2 Decision Trees

Another popular classification approach is the decision tree algorithm. It uses a tree-like model of decisions to classify data points. In R, we can implement decision trees using the `rpart` package:
```

```R
# Load necessary library library(rpart)

# Fit a decision tree model

tree_model <- rpart(passed_exam ~ hours_studied, data = data_class)

# Plot the tree plot(tree_model) text(tree_model)
```

We introduced the fundamentals of supervised learning, focusing on regression and classification. We explored linear regression, multiple linear regression, logistic regression, and decision trees, providing hands-on examples in R. Understanding these basics is crucial for anyone looking to delve deeper into artificial intelligence and machine learning.

Building and Evaluating ML Models with caret and tidymodels

In recent years, R has established itself as a powerful tool for data analysis and statistical computing, particularly in the field of machine learning (ML). Two of the most popular packages for building and evaluating ML models in R are `caret` and `tidymodels`. This chapter will provide a comprehensive overview of both packages, highlighting their features, functionalities, and best practices for building and evaluating machine learning models.

We will start with an introduction to both packages, followed by the steps to prepare data, build, and evaluate models. We will also discuss the process of hyperparameter tuning and the importance of model evaluation metrics.

Section 1: Overview of caret and tidymodels ### 1.1 The caret Package

The `caret` package, short for "Classification And REgression Training," is designed to streamline the process of training predictive models in R. It provides a unified interface for various machine learning algorithms, offering tools for data preprocessing, feature selection, and model evaluation.

Key Features of caret:

Model Training: Simplifies the model training process with a consistent interface for different algorithms.

Preprocessing Tools: Offers data preprocessing techniques such as normalization, centering, and imputation.

Resampling Methods: Provides various methods to partition datasets for training and validation.

Parameter Tuning: Supports hyperparameter tuning with grid search and random search. ### 1.2 The tidymodels Framework

The `tidymodels` framework, which is designed for integration with the tidyverse, offers an array of packages dedicated to modeling and machine learning tasks. The tidymodels philosophy emphasizes a pipeline approach for model training and evaluation, making code cleaner and more comprehensible.

Key Features of tidymodels:

Modular Design: Composed of multiple packages that can be combined seamlessly for different modeling tasks.

Tidy Data Principles: All functions accept and return data in the tidy format, making data manipulation intuitive.

Workflow System: Integrated workflows for model specification, fitting, and tuning.

Cross-validation: Built-in support for resampling and validation techniques. ## Section 2: Data Preparation

Building a robust machine learning model begins with thorough data preparation. Both `caret` and

`tidymodels` offer various features for preparing data.

2.1 Data Cleaning

Data cleaning involves handling missing values, correcting inconsistencies, and transforming variables. Let's explore data cleaning using both packages.

```r
# Using caret for data preprocessing library(caret)

data <- read.csv("data.csv")

data_clean <- na.omit(data) # Removing NA values

# Using tidymodels for data preprocessing library(tidymodels)

data_clean <- data %>% drop_na() # Removing NA values
```

2.2 Splitting the Data

Before training a model, it is essential to split data into training and testing sets.

```r
# Using caret set.seed(123)
trainIndex <- createDataPartition(data_clean$target, p = .8,
list = FALSE, times = 1)
train_data <- data_clean[trainIndex,] test_data <- data_clean[-trainIndex,]
# Using tidymodels set.seed(123)
data_split <- initial_split(data_clean, prop = 0.8)
train_data <- training(data_split)
test_data <- testing(data_split)
```

Section 3: Building Models

Once the data is prepared, we can proceed to build various machine learning models. ### 3.1 Model Training with caret

Let's utilize the `caret` package to train a random forest model.

```r
library(caret)
model_rf <- train(target ~ ., data = train_data, method = "rf", trControl = trainControl(method = "cv", number = 10))
```

3.2 Model Training with tidymodels

Now, let's achieve the same with `tidymodels`.

```r
library(tidymodels)

rf_spec <- rand_forest() %>% set_engine("ranger") %>%
set_mode("classification")

rf_workflow <- workflow() %>% add_model(rf_spec)
%>% add_formula(target ~ .)

rf_fit <- rf_workflow %>% fit(data = train_data)
```

Section 4: Model Evaluation

Once we have built our model, it is important to evaluate its performance. ### 4.1 Evaluation with caret

Using `caret`, we can easily evaluate the model's performance on the test data.

```r
predictions <- predict(model_rf, newdata = test_data)
confusionMatrix(predictions, test_data$target)
```

4.2 Evaluation with tidymodels

In `tidymodels`, we can evaluate the model in a more structured way.

```r
rf_results <- rf_fit %>% predict(new_data = test_data)
%>% bind_cols(test_data)
```

66

```r
metrics <- rf_results %>%
metrics(truth = target, estimate = .pred_class)
```

Section 5: Hyperparameter Tuning

Optimizing model performance through hyperparameter tuning is crucial. Both `caret` and `tidymodels` offer methods for tuning hyperparameters.

5.1 Tuning with caret

```r
tune_grid <- expand.grid(mtry = c(1, 2, 3),
splitrule = c("gini", "extratrees"), min.node.size = c(1, 5))
tuned_model <- train(target ~ ., data = train_data, method = "rf",
tuneGrid = tune_grid)
```

5.2 Tuning with tidymodels

```r
grid <- grid_regular(mtry(range = c(1, 6)), min_n(range = c(1, 10)), levels = 5)
tuned_rf <- rf_workflow %>%
tune_grid(resamples = vfold_cv(train_data, v = 5), grid = grid)
```

We have explored how to build and evaluate machine learning models using `caret` and `tidymodels` in R.

Both packages provide robust methods for model training, evaluation, and hyperparameter tuning. By understanding the strengths and specific use cases of each, data scientists can effectively leverage them to enhance their machine learning workflows. Whether choosing the comprehensive approach of `caret` or the tidy and modular philosophy of `tidymodels`, mastering these tools is crucial for any professional working in AI and machine learning in R.

Chapter 5: Advanced Machine Learning Techniques

In this chapter, we will explore advanced machine learning techniques available in R that are instrumental in building sophisticated AI models.

5.1 Overview of Machine Learning in R

Before diving into advanced techniques, it's essential to understand why R is an excellent choice for machine learning. R provides a wide array of libraries designed to simplify the process of data manipulation, visualization, and model building. Some of the most widely used libraries in the context of machine learning include:

caret: A unified interface for various machine learning algorithms.

randomForest: An implementation of the Random Forest algorithm for classification and regression.

xgboost: A powerful gradient boosting framework that has proven performance in predictive modeling.

keras: A high-level neural networks API, allowing for easy construction and training of deep learning models.

In this chapter, we will delve into several advanced machine learning techniques, including ensemble methods, support vector machines, deep learning, and natural language processing (NLP), all while leveraging the power of R.

5.2 Ensemble Methods

Ensemble methods combine multiple learning algorithms to achieve improved predictive performance. The most notable ensemble techniques include Bagging, Boosting, and Stacking.

5.2.1 Bagging

Bagging, or Bootstrap Aggregating, reduces variance by aggregating the predictions from multiple models. The Random Forest algorithm is a prime example, which constructs multiple decision trees and merges their predictions. Here's a simple implementation using the **randomForest** package in R:

```R
# Load necessary libraries library(randomForest)

# Load the iris dataset data(iris)

# Create a random forest model set.seed(123) # for reproducibility

rf_model <- randomForest(Species ~ ., data = iris, importance = TRUE)

# Print the model summary print(rf_model)


# Plot variable importance varImpPlot(rf_model)
```

5.2.2 Boosting

Boosting, such as AdaBoost or Gradient Boosting, works by sequentially training models, where each model attempts to correct the errors of the prior model. The **xgboost** package provides an efficient implementation for gradient boosting, which can be easily customized with various parameters.

```R
# Load the xgboost library library(xgboost)
```

Prepare data matrices

```
data_matrix <- xgb.DMatrix(data = as.matrix(iris[,-5]),
label = as.numeric(iris$Species) - 1)
```

Set parameters for gradient boosting

```
params <- list(objective = "multi:softprob", num_class =
3, eta = 0.1, max_depth = 6)
```

Train the model

```
xgb_model <- xgboost(data = data_matrix, params =
params, nrounds = 100)
```

Make predictions

```
pred <- predict(xgb_model, data_matrix)
```

5.2.3 Stacking

Stacking involves training a new model to aggregate the predictions from several base models. This meta-learning approach can significantly boost performance. Below is an example of stacking using the `caret` package:

```R
library(caret)
```

Define control using cross-validation

```
control <- trainControl(method = "cv", number = 5)
```

Train base models

```
model1 <- train(Species ~ ., data = iris, method = "rpart",
trControl = control) model2 <- train(Species ~ ., data =
iris, method = "rf", trControl = control)
```

Stack the models

```
stacked_model <- caretStack(list(model1, model2),
method = "glm")
```

5.3 Support Vector Machines

Support Vector Machines (SVM) are powerful classifiers that work well for both linear and non-linear data. They are particularly effective in high-dimensional spaces. In R, the **e1071** package provides a straightforward interface to implement SVM.

```R
library(e1071)

# Train an SVM model
svm_model <- svm(Species ~ ., data = iris, kernel = "linear")

# Predict on the training data predictions <- predict(svm_model, iris)

# Print the confusion matrix confusionMatrix(predictions, iris$Species)
```

5.4 Deep Learning with Keras

Deep learning has revolutionized the field of AI, enabling breakthroughs in image recognition, natural language understanding, and much more. The **keras** package makes it simple to build and train neural networks in R.

```R
library(keras)
```

```R
# Prepare the dataset
x_train <- as.matrix(iris[, 1:4])
y_train <- to_categorical(as.numeric(iris$Species) - 1)
# Build the model
model <- keras_model_sequential() %>%
layer_dense(units = 64, activation = "relu", input_shape =
ncol(x_train)) %>% layer_dropout(rate = 0.5) %>%
layer_dense(units = 3, activation = "softmax")
# Compile the model
model %>% compile(loss = "categorical_crossentropy",
optimizer = "adam", metrics = "accuracy")
# Train the model
model %>% fit(x_train, y_train, epochs = 50, batch_size
= 5)
```

5.5 Natural Language Processing (NLP)

In the age of big data, NLP has gained prominence for its ability to analyze text data. The **tm**,

tidytext, and **text2vec** packages in R provide tools for text mining, sentiment analysis, and topic modeling.

```R
R library(tm)
# Load text data
text_data <- Corpus(VectorSource(c("This is a good day", "I love programming in R", "Machine learning is fun")))
# Clean the text
```

```
text_data_clean        <-        tm_map(text_data,
content_transformer(tolower))    text_data_clean   <-
tm_map(text_data_clean,          removePunctuation)
text_data_clean        <-        tm_map(text_data_clean,
removeWords, stopwords("en"))
```

Create a Document-Term Matrix

```
dtm        <-        DocumentTermMatrix(text_data_clean)
inspect(dtm)
```
```

This chapter introduced some of the most advanced machine learning techniques available in R, enabling users to build sophisticated AI models. Whether employing ensemble methods, SVMs, deep learning frameworks, or exploring the rich field of NLP, R provides a comprehensive set of tools that can accommodate the intricacies of modern data science.

# Ensemble Methods: Random Forests, XGBoost, and Gradient Boosting

By leveraging the power of multiple models, ensemble methods can reduce overfitting, enhance accuracy, and increase robustness. This chapter delves into three prominent ensemble methods: Random Forests, XGBoost, and Gradient Boosting. We will explore their fundamental theories, practical implementations in R, and the contexts in which they thrive.

## 1. Understanding Ensemble Methods

Ensemble methods are machine learning strategies that combine multiple base models to create a single, stronger
```

predictive model. The underlying philosophy is that a group of weak learners can become a strong learner when combined. The two main types of ensemble methods are bagging and boosting.

1.1 Bagging

Bagging, or Bootstrap Aggregating, operates by training multiple models independently using different subsets of the training data. Each model provides a vote or prediction, and the final output is based on aggregating these individual predictions. Random Forests is a seminal example of a bagging approach.

1.2 Boosting

Boosting, on the other hand, is a sequential ensemble method where each model builds on the errors of its predecessors. It assigns weights to data points based on their prediction errors, focusing more on the harder- to-predict observations. XGBoost and Gradient Boosting are key algorithms under this umbrella.

2. Random Forests ### 2.1 Overview

Random Forests is an ensemble method that constructs multiple decision trees during training. It introduces randomness into the tree-building process, which enhances variance reduction and ultimately leads to strong predictions.

2.2 How Random Forests Work

Bootstrapping: Create multiple subsets of the original dataset by sampling with replacement.

Tree Construction: For each subset, build a decision tree using a random subset of features at each split.

Aggregation: The output predictions are obtained by averaging (for regression) or majority voting (for classification) from all the trees.

2.3 Implementation in R

To implement Random Forests in R, you can use the `randomForest` package. Here's a simple example:

```R
# Load the necessary library library(randomForest)

# Load the data data(iris)
# Train a Random Forest model set.seed(42)
rf_model <- randomForest(Species ~ ., data = iris, ntree = 100)
# Print the model summary print(rf_model)
# Make predictions
predictions <- predict(rf_model, iris)
# Evaluate accuracy table(predictions, iris$Species)
```

2.4 Advantages and Limitations
Advantages:

Handles both classification and regression tasks.

Automatically manages missing values.

Provides feature importance metrics.

Limitations:

Can be slow to predict due to a large number of trees.

Less interpretable compared to single decision trees. ## 3. Gradient Boosting

3.1 Overview

Gradient Boosting builds models sequentially; each new model attempts to correct the errors made by the previous one. By focusing on the residuals, it improves predictive performance significantly.

3.2 How Gradient Boosting Works

Initialization: Start with an initial prediction (often the mean).

Sequential Training: For a defined number of iterations, do the following:

Calculate the residuals (errors) from the previous model.

Train a weak learner (usually a shallow decision tree) on these residuals.

Update the predictions by adding the new model's predictions, multiplied by a learning rate. ### 3.3 Implementation in R

To implement Gradient Boosting in R, the `gbm` package is frequently used. Here's a simple example:

```R
# Load the library library(gbm)

# Load the data data(iris)
```

```
# Train a Gradient Boosting model set.seed(42)

gbm_model <- gbm(Species ~ ., data = iris, distribution =
"multinomial", n.trees = 100, interaction.depth = 3,
cv.folds = 5)

# Make predictions

predictions <- predict(gbm_model, iris, n.trees = 100,
type = "response") predictions <- max.col(predictions)

# Evaluate accuracy table(predictions, iris$Species)
```

3.4 Advantages and Limitations

Advantages:

Generally achieves higher accuracy than Random Forests, especially on structured/tabular data.

Flexible in customizing to various types of problems.

Limitations:

Can be prone to overfitting if not properly tuned.

Longer training time compared to bagging methods. ## 4. XGBoost

4.1 Overview

XGBoost (Extreme Gradient Boosting) is an optimized implementation of gradient boosting designed for speed and performance. It is particularly popular in competitive machine learning due to its efficiency and predictive power.

4.2 Key Features

Regularization: Incorporates L1 and L2 regularization

to prevent overfitting.

Parallel Processing: Takes advantage of multicore processors for faster computation.

Cross-Validation: Built-in cross-validation support to tune hyperparameters. ### 4.3 Implementation in R

For XGBoost, the `xgboost` package is the preferred choice. Here's a simple example:

```R
# Load the library library(xgboost)
# Prepare data: Convert to matrix format
data_matrix <- model.matrix(Species ~ . - 1, data = iris)
labels <- as.numeric(iris$Species) - 1  # Convert labels to numeric
# Train an XGBoost model set.seed(42)
dtrain <- xgb.DMatrix(data = data_matrix, label = labels)
xgb_model <- xgboost(dtrain, nrounds = 100, objective = "multi:softmax", num_class = 3)
# Make predictions
predictions <- predict(xgb_model, dtrain)
# Evaluate accuracy table(predictions, labels)
```

4.4 Advantages and Limitations

Advantages:

Exceptional speed and performance on large datasets.

Highly customizable with various hyperparameters to

79

tune.

State-of-the-art results in many prediction tasks.

Limitations:

Complexity in tuning hyperparameters can be daunting for beginners.

Potentially confusing application due to numerous parameters available.

Ensemble methods like Random Forests, Gradient Boosting, and XGBoost have revolutionized the field of machine learning, providing robust and accurate models for various tasks. By understanding their working principles and gaining proficiency in their application through R, data scientists and AI practitioners can significantly enhance their modeling capabilities. As the landscape of machine learning evolves, these ensemble techniques will continue to play a vital role in driving innovation and improving predictive performance across industries.

Model Tuning, Cross-Validation, and Performance Optimization

Model tuning, cross-validation, and performance optimization are critical steps in the machine learning workflow that help you derive the best results from your data. In this chapter, we will explore these topics using R—one of the most popular programming languages for statistical analysis and machine learning.

1. Understanding Model Tuning ### 1.1 What is Model Tuning?

Model tuning involves adjusting the hyperparameters of a machine learning model to enhance its performance. While model parameters are learned from the training data, hyperparameters are set before the training process and control various aspects of the model such as learning rate, depth of decision trees, number of neighbors (in KNN), and so on.

1.2 Common Hyperparameters in Popular Models

Decision Trees: Maximum depth, minimum samples per leaf

Random Forests: Number of trees, maximum depth, minimum samples per leaf

Support Vector Machines: Kernel type, regularization parameter (C)

Neural Networks: Learning rate, number of layers, number of neurons per layer ### 1.3 Techniques for Model Tuning

Model tuning can be conducted using several different techniques:

Grid Search: This method involves defining a grid of hyperparameter values and exhaustively evaluating all possible combinations to determine the best one.

Random Search: Unlike grid search, random search randomly samples parameter combinations and requires significantly less computation.

Bayesian Optimization: Provides a more efficient approach by building a probabilistic model of the loss function and choosing hyperparameters that optimize the expected improvement.

Example: Grid Search in R

```R
R library(caret)
# Define the model and parameters
model <- trainControl(method = "cv", number = 10) grid <- expand.grid(mtry = seq(1, 10, 1))
# Train the model using Grid Search
tuned_model <- train(Species ~ ., data = iris, method = "rf", trControl = model, tuneGrid = grid) print(tuned_model)
```

2. Cross-Validation

2.1 What is Cross-Validation?

Cross-validation is a technique used to assess the generalizability of a model. It helps estimate how a predictive model will perform in practice when applied to unseen data. The key idea is to split the data into several subsets or folds.

2.2 K-Fold Cross-Validation

In K-fold cross-validation, the dataset is divided into 'K' subsets or folds. The model is trained on 'K-1' folds and validated on the remaining fold. This process is repeated 'K' times, with each fold serving as the validation set once. The results are then averaged to provide an overall performance metric.

Example: K-Fold Cross-Validation in R

```R
R set.seed(123)
control <- trainControl(method="cv", number=10)
```

```
model <- train(Species ~ ., data=iris, method="rf",
trControl=control) print(model)
```
` ` `

3. Performance Optimization

3.1 Evaluating Model Performance

After tuning the model and validating it, the next step is to
evaluate its performance using various metrics depending
on the type of problem you are solving.

Classification Metrics: Accuracy, Precision, Recall, F1
Score, ROC-AUC

Regression Metrics: Mean Absolute Error (MAE),
Mean Squared Error (MSE), R^2 Score ### 3.2
Performance Optimization Techniques

3.2.1 Feature Engineering

Improving feature selection and engineering can
significantly enhance model performance. Techniques
include:

Normalization/Standardization: Scaling features can
lead to better training outcomes.

Dimensionality Reduction: Algorithms like PCA
(Principal Component Analysis) can help in reducing the
feature set without significant loss of information.

3.2.2 Ensemble Techniques

Combining multiple models can often yield better
accuracy. Techniques like bagging, boosting, and stacking
can be employed.

Example: Random Forest as an Ensemble Method in

R

```R
library(randomForest) set.seed(123)

rf_model <- randomForest(Species ~ ., data=iris, ntree=100) print(rf_model)
```

Model tuning, cross-validation, and performance optimization are indispensable components of the machine learning lifecycle. These processes not only help enhance the accuracy of predictions but also ensure that the models can generalize well to unseen data. By leveraging techniques available in R, data scientists and AI practitioners can significantly improve their models' performance, paving the way for more reliable and effective applications in real-world scenarios.

Chapter 6: Introduction to Deep Learning with R

Deep learning represents a significant leap in the field of artificial intelligence (AI), leveraging vast amounts of data to create powerful models that can learn complex patterns and make predictions or decisions without explicit programming. In this chapter, we will dive into the world of deep learning using R, a language renowned for its statistical capabilities and data manipulation strengths. By harnessing the power of R, we can build sophisticated neural networks, analyze their performance, and apply them to real-world problems.

6.1 Understanding Deep Learning

Deep learning is a subset of machine learning that utilizes neural networks with many layers (hence the term "deep"). Unlike traditional machine learning methods—where feature extraction is typically the responsibility of the developer—deep learning automatically discovers features from the raw data, enabling a more direct relationship between inputs and outputs.

Key Concepts in Deep Learning

Neural Networks: Composed of layers of interconnected nodes (neurons), each layer transforms the input data, extracting increasingly complex features. The architecture of a neural network determines its capacity and performance.

Activation Functions: These functions introduce non-linearities into the model, allowing it to learn complex patterns. Common activation functions include ReLU (Rectified Linear Unit), Sigmoid, and Tanh.

Loss Functions: To train a neural network, we define a loss function that measures how well the model's predictions match the actual outcomes. The goal is to minimize this loss during training.

Backpropagation: This algorithm is used for training the neural networks. It calculates the gradient of the loss function with respect to the weights of the network, allowing the model to adjust its parameters to improve accuracy.

Optimization: Techniques like Stochastic Gradient Descent (SGD) and Adam are employed to update the weights of the neural network based on the gradients computed during backpropagation.

6.2 Setting Up the R Environment for Deep Learning

To begin our deep learning journey in R, we must set up our environment. The most popular packages for deep learning include:

Keras: An R interface to the Keras Python library, Keras allows for the building, training, and evaluating of deep learning models in a straightforward manner.

TensorFlow: As the backend engine behind Keras, TensorFlow enables complex computations essential for deep learning.

caret: While not specific to deep learning, the caret package is useful for model training and evaluation.

Installation

To get started, first install the required packages:

```R
install.packages("keras")
library(keras)
```

Make sure TensorFlow is installed as well:

```R
keras::install_keras()
```

6.3 Building Your First Neural Network in R

Now that our environment is set up, let's build a simple neural network model using the Keras package. In this example, we will use the classic MNIST dataset, which contains handwritten digits.

Loading the Data

First, we need to load the MNIST dataset available through Keras:

```R
mnist <- dataset_mnist()
x_train <- mnist$train$x
y_train <- mnist$train$y
x_test <- mnist$test$x
y_test <- mnist$test$y
```

Data Preprocessing

Before feeding the data into our model, we need to preprocess it:

Normalize pixel values to the range [0, 1].

Reshape the data from 3D arrays to 2D matrices.

Convert labels to categorical format.

```R
```

```R
x_train <- x_train / 255 x_test <- x_test / 255

x_train <- array_reshape(x_train, c(nrow(x_train), 28 *
28)) x_test <- array_reshape(x_test, c(nrow(x_test), 28 *
28))

y_train <- to_categorical(y_train, num_classes = 10)
y_test <- to_categorical(y_test, num_classes = 10)
```

Creating the Model

We can now define a simple feedforward neural network
using Keras:

```R
model <- keras_model_sequential() %>%

layer_dense(units = 128, activation = 'relu', input_shape =
c(28 * 28)) %>% layer_dropout(rate = 0.2) %>%


layer_dense(units = 10, activation = 'softmax')
```

Compiling the Model

Next, we must compile our model by specifying the
optimizer, loss function, and metrics:

```R
model %>% compile(

loss = 'categorical_crossentropy', optimizer = 'adam',

metrics = c('accuracy')

)
```

```
```

Training the Model

We can now train the model using the training dataset:

```R
model %>% fit( x_train, y_train, epochs = 5,
batch_size = 32,
validation_split = 0.2
)
```

Evaluating the Model

After training, we can evaluate the model on the test dataset to gauge its performance:

```R
score <- model %>% evaluate(x_test, y_test) cat('Test loss:', score$loss, "\n")
cat('Test accuracy:', score$acc, "\n")
```

6.4 Improving the Model

While the model we built is functional, there are several ways to enhance its performance:

Layer Architecture: Experiment with deeper networks or different layer types, such as convolutional layers for image data.

Regularization Methods: Techniques like dropout and L2 regularization help reduce overfitting.

89

Hyperparameter Tuning: Adjust learning rates, batch sizes, and the number of epochs for better optimization.

6.5 Use Cases of Deep Learning in R

Deep learning can be applied to various domains, including:

Image Recognition: Applications in security systems and autonomous vehicles.

Natural Language Processing: Used in chatbots, translation services, and sentiment analysis.

Forecasting: Time series predictions in finance, weather, and supply chain management.

Deep learning in R is an accessible yet powerful approach to tackling complex AI problems. Through this chapter, we have introduced the fundamental concepts of deep learning, set up our R environment, and built a basic neural network model. As the field continues to grow, the ecosystem around deep learning in R will evolve, offering even more tools and techniques for developers and data scientists to explore.

Understanding Neural Networks and Deep Learning Concepts

This chapter aims to demystify neural networks and deep learning concepts, focusing on their implementation in R, a powerful programming language for statistical computing and graphics. We will explore the fundamentals of neural networks, delve into how deep learning builds on these foundations, and provide practical examples to illustrate their application using R.

1. The Basics of Neural Networks ### 1.1 What is a Neural Network?

A neural network is a computational model inspired by the way biological neural networks in the human brain process information. It consists of interconnected nodes, or neurons, organized in layers:

Input Layer: Takes the features of the data as input.

Hidden Layer(s): Processes inputs through weighted connections. The number of hidden layers and neurons can vary, which influences the network's capacity to learn complex patterns.

Output Layer: Produces the final prediction or classification based on the processed input. ### 1.2 Key Components

Neurons: The fundamental units of a neural network, each receiving signals from the previous layer, applying a transformation, and sending signals to the next layer.

Weights and Biases: Each connection between neurons has an associated weight that scales the signal; a bias allows the model to fit the data even when all inputs are zero.

Activation Functions: These functions introduce non-linearity to the model, enabling it to learn complex relationships. Common activation functions include ReLU (Rectified Linear Unit), Sigmoid, and Tanh.

1.3 Forward Pass and Backpropagation

The learning process in a neural network involves two main steps:

Forward Pass: Inputs are passed through the network

91

layer by layer to produce an output.

Backpropagation: The error between the predicted output and the actual output is calculated. The network then adjusts its weights and biases to minimize this error using optimization techniques like gradient descent.

2. Introduction to Deep Learning ### 2.1 What is Deep Learning?

Deep learning refers to neural networks with multiple hidden layers, enabling them to learn hierarchical representations of data. While traditional neural networks can solve basic problems, deep learning excels in handling large amounts of data and complex tasks such as image and speech recognition.

2.2 The Power of Deep Learning

Deep learning has revolutionized various fields by leveraging large datasets and powerful computational resources. The architecture of deep neural networks allows them to automatically extract features from raw data, reducing the need for manual feature engineering.

3. Implementing Neural Networks in R ### 3.1 Setting Up Your Environment

To get started with neural networks in R, ensure you have the necessary packages installed. Key libraries to consider are:

keras: An R interface to Keras, a deep learning framework that enables you to build and train neural networks.

tensorflow: The backend engine for Keras, providing powerful capabilities for numerical computation.

nnet: A basic package for creating feedforward neural networks.

You can install these packages using the following commands in your R console:

```R
install.packages("keras") install.packages("nnet")
```

3.2 Creating a Simple Neural Network

Let's build a basic neural network using the `keras` library. Here, we will implement a model to classify the famous MNIST dataset of handwritten digits.

```R
library(keras)

# Load and preprocess the data mnist <- dataset_mnist()

x_train <- array_reshape(mnist$train$x, c(nrow(mnist$train$x), 28 * 28)) x_train <- x_train / 255 # Normalize

y_train <- to_categorical(mnist$train$y, 10)

# Define the model

model <- keras_model_sequential() %>%

layer_dense(units = 128, activation = 'relu', input_shape = c(28 * 28)) %>% layer_dropout(rate = 0.2) %>%

layer_dense(units = 10, activation = 'softmax')

# Compile the model model %>% compile(

loss = 'categorical_crossentropy', optimizer = 'adam',

metrics = c('accuracy')

)
```

```
# Train the model
model %>% fit(x_train, y_train, epochs = 5, batch_size = 32)
```

3.3 Evaluating the Model

Once the model is trained, you can evaluate its performance on the test dataset:

```R
x_test <- array_reshape(mnist$test$x, c(nrow(mnist$test$x), 28 * 28)) x_test <- x_test / 255

y_test <- to_categorical(mnist$test$y, 10)

model %>% evaluate(x_test, y_test)
```

4. Advanced Concepts in Deep Learning

4.1 Convolutional Neural Networks (CNNs)

For tasks involving image data, Convolutional Neural Networks (CNNs) are particularly powerful. CNNs employ convolutional layers that automatically learn spatial hierarchies of features. They are the backbone of most state-of-the-art models for image classification tasks.

4.2 Recurrent Neural Networks (RNNs)

Recurrent Neural Networks (RNNs) are designed for sequential data, such as time series or natural language. RNNs maintain a hidden state that carries information from one input to the next, allowing them to capture temporal dependencies.

4.3 Transfer Learning

Transfer learning is the practice of taking a pre-trained model on one task and fine-tuning it for a different but related task. This approach significantly reduces training time and improves performance, especially when labeled data is scarce.

Neural networks and deep learning are transformative forces driving advancements in AI across various fields. Understanding the underlying concepts and how to implement them in R equips you with the tools needed to harness the power of AI. As the technology continues to evolve, further exploration into specialized architectures and techniques will unlock new possibilities. Embrace the learning journey, and become part of the revolution that neural networks and deep learning are bringing to the world.

Implementing Deep Learning with the keras and tensor flow Packages

In R, the Keras and TensorFlow packages provide powerful tools for constructing and training deep learning models. This chapter aims to guide you through the process of implementing deep learning models in R using these two packages, providing a comprehensive overview of their functionalities, features, and practical applications.

Setting Up Your Environment

Before beginning with deep learning, it is essential to set up your R environment. You will need to install Keras and

TensorFlow. The following code snippets will help you install the necessary packages:

```R
# Install the required packages
install.packages("tensorflow") install.packages("keras")

# Load the packages library(tensorflow) library(keras)

# Install TensorFlow backend
tensorflow::install_tensorflow()
```

This will ensure that both TensorFlow and Keras are installed and properly configured in your R environment. The Keras package in R serves as an interface to the TensorFlow library, making it easier to construct and train deep learning models.

Understanding Keras and TensorFlow

Keras is a high-level neural networks API that allows users to build and train deep learning models easily. Built on top of TensorFlow, Keras provides a user-friendly approach for experimenting with various neural network architectures. TensorFlow, on the other hand, is a low-level library that offers greater flexibility and scalability for building complex machine learning models.

Constructing a Deep Learning Model

In this section, we will go through the steps of constructing a basic deep learning model using Keras for a classification problem, namely, the MNIST dataset of handwritten digits. The goal will be to create a neural network capable of recognizing digits from 0 to 9.

Loading Data

First, let's load the MNIST dataset and preprocess it:

```R
# Load the MNIST dataset mnist <- dataset_mnist()


# Split data into training and test sets x_train <- mnist$train$x

y_train <- mnist$train$y x_test <- mnist$test$x y_test <- mnist$test$y

# Reshape and normalize the images

x_train <- array_reshape(x_train, c(nrow(x_train), 28, 28, 1))

x_test <- array_reshape(x_test, c(nrow(x_test), 28, 28, 1)) x_train <- x_train / 255

x_test <- x_test / 255

# Convert labels to categorical format y_train <- to_categorical(y_train, 10) y_test <- to_categorical(y_test, 10)
```

Building the Model

Now that the data is preprocessed, let's build the neural network model:

```R
# Define the model architecture

model <- keras_model_sequential() %>%
```

```R
layer_conv_2d(filters = 32, kernel_size = c(3, 3),
activation = "relu", input_shape = c(28, 28, 1)) %>%
layer_max_pooling_2d(pool_size = c(2, 2)) %>%

layer_flatten() %>%

layer_dense(units = 128, activation = "relu") %>%
layer_dense(units = 10, activation = "softmax")

# Compile the model model %>% compile(

loss = "categorical_crossentropy", optimizer = "adam",

metrics = c("accuracy")

)
```

Training the Model

With the model built, we can proceed to train it using the training dataset:

```R
# Train the model

history <- model %>% fit( x_train, y_train,

epochs = 10,

batch_size = 128,

validation_split = 0.2

)
```

Evaluating the Model

After training, it is crucial to evaluate the model's performance on the test set:

```R
# Evaluate the model

score <- model %>% evaluate(x_test, y_test) cat("Test
loss:", score$loss, "\n")

cat("Test accuracy:", score$acc, "\n")
```

Fine-Tuning Your Model

To enhance the performance of your model, consider
experimenting with hyperparameter tuning, such as
adjusting the learning rate, changing the number of layers,
or modifying the number of neurons in each layer. Keras
provides optimized functions for this purpose, including
callbacks for early stopping and learning rate reduction.

```R
# Implement early stopping

early_stopping <- callback_early_stopping(monitor =
"val_loss", patience = 3)

# Retrain the model with early stopping history <- model
%>% fit(

x_train, y_train, epochs = 50,

batch_size = 128,

validation_split = 0.2, callbacks = list(early_stopping)

)
```

Saving and Loading Models

Once satisfied with the model's performance, you may

want to save it for future use. Keras provides an easy way to save and load models:

```R
# Save the model
model %>% save_model_hdf5("mnist_model.h5")
# Load the model
loaded_model <- load_model_hdf5("mnist_model.h5")
```

Deep learning applications using Keras and TensorFlow in R are vast and varied. Industries such as healthcare, finance, robotics, and e-commerce leverage deep learning for tasks like predictive analytics, sentiment analysis, fraud detection, and more. By understanding the foundational principles of building and training deep learning models in R, you can apply your knowledge to solve real-world problems.

In this chapter, we have covered the essential steps for implementing deep learning models using Keras and TensorFlow in R. From setting up the environment and loading data to building, training, evaluating, and saving models, you now have the foundational knowledge to embark on your deep learning journey.

Chapter 7: Building and Training Neural Networks

This chapter focuses on the practical aspects of building and training neural networks using R, a language well-suited for statistical computing and data analysis. We will explore the fundamental concepts of neural networks, the necessary libraries in R, and a hands-on approach to constructing and training a neural network model.

Understanding Neural Networks

At their core, neural networks are computational models inspired by the human brain's interconnected network of neurons. They are composed of layers of nodes (or neurons), where each layer transforms the input data through weighted connections. Typically, a neural network consists of an input layer, one or more hidden layers, and an output layer.

Key Terminology

Neurons: The basic units of a neural network that receive input, apply a function, and output a result.

Layers: Groups of neurons. The input layer receives raw data, hidden layers perform transformation, and the output layer provides the final prediction.

Weights and Biases: Parameters that are adjusted during training. They influence the strength and direction of the connections between neurons.

Activation Functions: Functions applied to the weighted sums of inputs that introduce non-linearity to the model. Common activation functions include ReLU, sigmoid, and tanh.

Setting Up the R Environment ### Necessary Libraries

To build and train neural networks in R, we will primarily use the `keras` and `tensorflow` libraries. The Keras package provides a high-level interface to build neural networks, while TensorFlow serves as a backend engine for running computations.

First, you need to install the necessary libraries. In R, you can do this by running:

```R
install.packages("keras") library(keras)
```

After installing Keras, you may also need to install TensorFlow. You can install it using the following command:

```R
install_keras()
```

This command will download and install the TensorFlow package along with necessary configurations. ## Building a Neural Network in R

Defining the Model

Now that our environment is set, let's define a simple feedforward neural network for a classification task using the well-known Iris dataset. We will predict the species of iris flowers based on features like sepal length, sepal width, petal length, and petal width.

```R
# Load the dataset data(iris)
```

```
# Convert the species variable to a one-hot encoded matrix
iris$Species <- as.numeric(factor(iris$Species)) - 1
```

```
x <- as.matrix(iris[, 1:4])
```

```
y <- to_categorical(iris$Species)
```

```
# Split the dataset into training and testing sets
set.seed(123) # For reproducibility
```

```
indices <- sample(1:nrow(iris), size = 0.8 * nrow(iris))
x_train <- x[indices, ]
```

```
y_train <- y[indices, ] x_test <- x[-indices, ] y_test <- y[-indices, ]
```
` ` `

Creating the Neural Network Architecture

Using Keras, we can easily define our neural network structure. For our example, we will use one hidden layer with 10 neurons and ReLU as the activation function.

` ` `R

```
# Build the model
```

```
model <- keras_model_sequential() %>%
```

```
layer_dense(units = 10, activation = 'relu', input_shape = c(4)) %>% layer_dense(units = 3, activation = 'softmax') # Output layer for 3 classes
```
` ` `

Compiling the Model

Before training the model, we need to compile it by specifying a loss function, optimizer, and metrics for evaluation.

103

```R
model %>%

compile(loss = 'categorical_crossentropy', optimizer = optimizer_adam(), metrics = c('accuracy'))
```

Training the Model

We will fit our model to the training data over several epochs, allowing it to learn the underlying patterns in the dataset.

```R
history <- model %>% fit(x_train, y_train,

epochs = 100,

batch_size = 5,

validation_split = 0.2)
```

Evaluating the Model

After training, it's essential to evaluate the model's performance on the test set to ensure its generalization.

```R
score <- model %>% evaluate(x_test, y_test) cat('Test loss:', score$loss, '\n')

cat('Test accuracy:', score$accuracy, '\n')
```

Visualizing the Training Process
104

Visualization can help in understanding how well the model is learning. We can plot the training and validation accuracy over epochs to see if the model is overfitting.

```R
library(ggplot2)

# Convert history to a data frame history_df <- as.data.frame(history)

# Plot accuracy
ggplot(history_df, aes(x = epoch)) +

geom_line(aes(y = accuracy, color = 'Training Accuracy')) + geom_line(aes(y = val_accuracy, color = 'Validation Accuracy')) + ggtitle('Model Accuracy') +

xlab('Epochs') + ylab('Accuracy') +

scale_color_manual(values = c('blue', 'red'))
```

We navigated through the process of building and training a neural network in R. We covered the tools necessary, constructed a basic model, trained it using a real dataset, and evaluated its performance. While this example was straightforward and intended for introductory purposes, the concepts and techniques explored here lay the groundwork for more complex and advanced neural network applications in various fields.

Designing Multilayer Perceptrons for Classification Tasks

The nodes in these networks use activation functions to transform their inputs into outputs, enabling the network to learn complex patterns and relationships in data.

In this chapter, we will explore how to design, train, and evaluate MLPs for classification tasks using R, a powerful programming language and environment for statistical computing and graphics. The focus will be on practical implementation, supported by theoretical insights to enhance your understanding of the underlying mechanics of MLPs.

Understanding the Architecture of MLPs An MLP is structured as follows:

Input Layer: This layer represents the features of the input data. Each node corresponds to one feature.

Hidden Layers: These layers perform intermediate computations and can be adjusted in number and size based on the complexity of the task.

Output Layer: This layer consists of nodes representing the classes or categories the model is predicting.

Each connection between nodes has an associated weight that is adjusted during the training process through a method called backpropagation.

Activation Functions

Activation functions introduce non-linearity into the model, allowing it to learn complex patterns. Common activation functions used in MLPs include:

Sigmoid: A function that transforms inputs into a value between 0 and 1, often used in binary classification.

ReLU (Rectified Linear Unit): Defined as $f(x) = \max(0, x)$, it helps mitigate the vanishing gradient problem and is favored for hidden layers in deep networks.

Softmax: Often used in the output layer of multi-class classification problems, it converts raw scores into probabilities that sum to one.

Designing an MLP in R

To develop an MLP for classification tasks, we will leverage the `keras` library in R. This library provides an intuitive interface for building deep learning models. Below are the step-by-step instructions for designing an MLP using the popular Iris dataset.

Step 1: Setting Up the Environment

First, ensure you have the necessary libraries installed. You can install them if not already done:

```r
install.packages("keras") library(keras)
```

Step 2: Load and Preprocess the Data

Let's load the Iris dataset and preprocess it for training.

```r
# Load the dataset data(iris)
```

Convert species to a categorical variable

iris$Species <- as.numeric(factor(iris$Species)) - 1 # 0, 1, 2

Splitting data into features and labels x <- as.matrix(iris[, 1:4]) # Features

```r
y <- to_categorical(iris$Species, num_classes = 3)  #
One-hot encoding for labels
# Split the data into training and testing sets set.seed(123)
train_indices <- sample(1:nrow(iris), 0.7 * nrow(iris))
x_train <- x[train_indices, ]
y_train <- y[train_indices, ] x_test <- x[-train_indices, ]
y_test <- y[-train_indices, ]
```

Step 3: Build the MLP Model

Now we will define the architecture of the MLP.

```r
model <- keras_model_sequential() %>%
layer_dense(units = 10, activation = 'relu', input_shape =
ncol(x_train)) %>% layer_dense(units = 10, activation =
'relu') %>%
layer_dense(units = 3, activation = 'softmax')  # Output
layer for 3 classes
```

Step 4: Compile the Model

Next, we compile the model, specifying the optimizer, loss
function, and metrics to evaluate.

```r
model %>% compile( optimizer = 'adam',
loss = 'categorical_crossentropy', metrics = c('accuracy')
)
```

```
```

Step 5: Train the Model

We can now train the model on the training data.

```r
history <- model %>% fit( x_train, y_train,
epochs = 100,
batch_size = 5,
validation_split = 0.2
)
```

Step 6: Evaluate the Model

After training the model, we evaluate its performance with the test set.

```r
score <- model %>% evaluate(x_test, y_test) cat('Test loss:', score$loss, "\n")
cat('Test accuracy:', score$accuracy, "\n")
```

Step 7: Making Predictions

Finally, we can make predictions on new data.

```r
predictions <- model %>% predict(x_test)
predicted_classes <- which.max(predictions, 2) - 1  #
```

Convert to class labels

```
```

Multilayer Perceptrons are powerful tools for classification tasks, capable of learning complex patterns within the data. In this chapter, we designed an MLP using R's `keras` package to classify the Iris dataset. By understanding the architecture, preprocessing data, and implementing the steps to train and evaluate a model, you are now equipped with the foundational knowledge to tackle other classification problems using MLPs in R.

Convolutional and Recurrent Neural Networks in R

In this chapter, we will explore both CNNs and RNNs, focusing on their implementation within the R programming environment. We will discuss their architectures, applications, and provide practical examples to illustrate their use in real-world AI problems.

1. Fundamentals of Neural Networks

Before delving into CNNs and RNNs, it's crucial to have a foundational understanding of neural networks. A neural network is composed of layers of interconnected nodes, or neurons, where each connection has an associated weight. The network learns patterns in the data through a process called training, which adjusts these weights based on the input and the expected output.

Neural networks rely on activation functions to introduce non-linearity, allowing the model to learn complex relationships. Common activation functions include ReLU

(Rectified Linear Unit), Sigmoid, and Tanh.

2. Convolutional Neural Networks (CNNs) ### 2.1 Overview

CNNs are specifically designed to process data with a grid-like topology, most commonly images. They leverage convolutional layers, pooling layers, and fully connected layers to learn spatial hierarchies of features from input data.

2.2 Architecture of CNNs

Convolutional Layer: This layer applies convolutional operations, where filters (or kernels) slide over the input data to extract features such as edges and textures. Each filter generates a feature map that highlights certain aspects of the input.

Activation Function: After convolution, an activation function is applied to introduce non-linearity. ReLU is commonly used in CNNs due to its efficiency and effectiveness in addressing the vanishing gradient problem.

Pooling Layer: This layer reduces the spatial dimensions of the input, summarizing the features detected in the previous layer. Max pooling and average pooling are popular techniques.

Fully Connected Layer: At the end of the network, fully connected layers combine features learned from the previous layers to produce final predictions.

2.3 Applications of CNNs

CNNs excel in various applications, including:

Image classification (e.g., identifying objects in photos)

Object detection (e.g., locating specific items within an image)

Image segmentation (e.g., separating different objects in an image)

Medical image analysis (e.g., diagnosing diseases from X-rays or MRIs)

2.4 Implementing CNNs in R

To implement a CNN in R, we can utilize the `keras` package, which provides a high-level neural networks API. Here's a basic example of building a CNN for image classification using the CIFAR-10 dataset:

```R
library(keras)

# Load CIFAR-10 dataset cifar10 <- dataset_cifar10()
x_train <- cifar10$train$x / 255

y_train <- to_categorical(cifar10$train$y, num_classes = 10) x_test <- cifar10$test$x / 255

y_test <- to_categorical(cifar10$test$y, num_classes = 10)

# Define the CNN model

model <- keras_model_sequential() %>%

layer_conv_2d(filters = 32, kernel_size = c(3, 3), activation = 'relu', input_shape = c(32, 32, 3)) %>%
layer_max_pooling_2d(pool_size = c(2, 2)) %>%

layer_conv_2d(filters = 64, kernel_size = c(3, 3), activation = 'relu') %>%
layer_max_pooling_2d(pool_size = c(2, 2)) %>%

layer_flatten() %>%
```

```
layer_dense(units = 128, activation = 'relu') %>%
layer_dense(units = 10, activation = 'softmax')
```

Compile the model

```
model %>% compile(loss = 'categorical_crossentropy',
optimizer = 'adam',

metrics = c('accuracy'))
```

Train the model

```
model %>% fit(x_train, y_train, epochs = 10, batch_size
= 64, validation_split = 0.2)
```

Evaluate the model

```
score <- model %>% evaluate(x_test, y_test) cat('Test
accuracy:', score$accuracy)
```
```
```

3. Recurrent Neural Networks (RNNs) ### 3.1 Overview

RNNs are designed to process sequential data, where current inputs depend on previous inputs. This architecture allows RNNs to maintain a hidden state that captures information from preceding time steps, making them ideal for tasks like language modeling and time series forecasting.

3.2 Architecture of RNNs

RNNs consist of recurrent layers that feed the output from previous time steps back into the network. Variants like Long Short-Term Memory (LSTM) networks and Gated Recurrent Units (GRUs) address limitations of vanilla RNNs, such as the vanishing gradient problem, enhancing their ability to learn long-term dependencies.

3.3 Applications of RNNs

NNs find applications in various fields, including:

Natural language processing (e.g., language translation, sentiment analysis)

Time series prediction (e.g., stock price forecasting)

Speech recognition (e.g., converting spoken language into text)

Video analysis (e.g., action detection) ### 3.4 Implementing RNNs in R

To implement an RNN in R with LSTM networks, we will use the same `keras` package. Here's an example for predicting the next word in a sequence:

```R
```R library(keras)
# Example text data

texts <- c("I love deep learning", "Deep learning is fascinating", "I enjoy programming in R") tokenizer <- text_tokenizer(num_words = 1000)

tokenizer %>% fit_text_tokenizer(texts)

# Convert texts to sequences sequences <- texts %>%

tokenizer$texts_to_sequences(tokenizer) max_length <- max(sapply(sequences, length))

# Padding sequences

padded_sequences <- pad_sequences(sequences, maxlen = max_length)

# Define the RNN model
```
```

```
model_rnn <- keras_model_sequential() %>%

layer_embedding(input_dim = 1000, output_dim = 128,
input_length = max_length) %>% layer_lstm(units = 64)
%>%

layer_dense(units = 1000, activation = 'softmax')

# Compile the model

model_rnn          %>%          compile(loss          =
'sparse_categorical_crossentropy', optimizer = 'adam',

metrics = c('accuracy'))

# (Skipping the training part for brevity; code would vary
based on the training dataset)
```
```

CNNs and RNNs represent powerful tools in the realm of
AI, each tailored to handle distinct types of data. In this
chapter, we explored their architectures, applications, and
implementations using R. The examples provided a
practical insight into how these networks can be employed
to solve real-world problems. As the field of AI continues
to evolve, mastering these architectures will be essential
for aspiring data scientists and AI practitioners aiming to
develop sophisticated applications.
```

Chapter 8: Natural Language Processing (NLP) with R

This chapter will explore how to implement NLP using R, a language and environment widely used for statistical computing and graphics.

Overview of NLP Concepts

Before diving into the practical implementation, we must first understand some fundamental concepts in NLP:

Text Preprocessing: The first step in any NLP task is to clean and preprocess the text data. This includes activities like removing punctuation, converting text to lowercase, tokenization (splitting text into individual words or tokens), and removing stop words (common words that add little meaning).

Tokenization: This process involves breaking text into smaller pieces, typically words or phrases, which can then be analyzed.

Term Frequency-Inverse Document Frequency (TF-IDF): This numerical statistic reflects the importance of a word in a document relative to a collection of documents (corpus).

Part-of-Speech (POS) Tagging: This assigns parts of speech to each word (noun, verb, adjective, etc.), allowing for a better understanding of grammatical structures.

Sentiment Analysis: This entails determining the sentiment expressed in a piece of text, which can be classified typically as positive, negative, or neutral.

Named Entity Recognition (NER): This aims to

identify and classify key entities within the text into predefined categories like names of people, organizations, locations, etc.

Word Embeddings: Techniques like Word2Vec and GloVe convert words into numerical vectors, capturing contextual meanings and relationships between words.

Getting Started with R for NLP

To harness the power of NLP in R, we need to install and load some essential packages. The most widely used libraries for NLP include `tm`, `text`, `quanteda`, and `stringr`.

```r
install.packages(c("tm", "text", "quanteda", "stringr"))
library(tm)

library(text) library(quanteda) library(stringr)
```

Sample Data

For demonstration purposes, we will work with a sample dataset comprising tweets. Let's say we want to analyze the sentiment of these tweets about a specific brand or topic.

```r
tweets <- c("I love the new features of the product!", "Horrible customer service experience.", "The quality could be better.")
```

Text Preprocessing

The first step is to preprocess our tweets. This includes converting text to lowercase, removing punctuation, and splitting the text into words.

```r
# Convert to lowercase tweets <- tolower(tweets)

# Remove punctuation
tweets <- gsub("[[:punct:]]+", "", tweets)
# Tokenization
tokens <- unlist(strsplit(tweets, "\\s+"))
```

Removing Stop Words

Next, we remove common stop words that do not contribute to the meaning of the text.

```r
# Load stop words data("stopwords", package = "tm")
tokens <- tokens[!tokens %in% stopwords("en")]
```

Term Frequency-Inverse Document Frequency (TF-IDF) Now, let's compute the TF-IDF values of the processed tokens.

```r
# Create a document term matrix
dtm                                              <-
DocumentTermMatrix(Corpus(VectorSource(tweets)))
```

118

```r
# Calculate TF-IDF
tfidf <- weightTfIdf(dtm)
```

Sentiment Analysis

Using the `text` package, we can perform sentiment analysis. R offers various methods for sentiment analysis, including lexicon-based approaches, which use predefined dictionaries of words associated with positive or negative sentiments.

```r
# Perform sentiment analysis
sentiment_scores <- text::textEmbed(text = tweets, model = 'sentiment', model_type = 'fasttext')
```

Named Entity Recognition (NER)

NER can be effectively implemented using the `text` and `quanteda` packages in R.

```r
# Identify entities
ner_results <- text::textEmbed(text = tweets, model = 'ner')
```

Visualization of Results

Visualizing the results can provide deeper insights. We can use libraries like `ggplot2` for this purpose.

````r
```r library(ggplot2)

# Example of plotting sentiment scores

sentiment_df <- data.frame(Tweet = tweets, Sentiment =
sentiment_scores) ggplot(sentiment_df, aes(x = Tweet, y
= Sentiment)) +

geom_bar(stat = "identity") +

theme(axis.text.x = element_text(angle = 45, hjust = 1)) +

labs(title = "Sentiment Analysis of Tweets", y =
"Sentiment Score")
```
````

We have introduced the fundamental concepts of NLP and demonstrated how to perform various NLP tasks using R. From text preprocessing through sentiment analysis and NER, R provides a rich set of tools that makes NLP accessible and powerful. As you delve deeper into R's capabilities and NLP techniques, you will uncover a world of possibilities to analyze and interpret textual data.

Text Mining, Tokenization, and Sentiment Analysis

Text mining, tokenization, and sentiment analysis are key techniques in this domain, enabling the extraction of meaningful insights from unstructured text. R, with its rich ecosystem of packages designed for statistical analysis and data visualization, serves as an excellent platform for performing these tasks in artificial intelligence (AI) applications. This chapter delves into the fundamentals of text mining, the process of tokenization, and how to conduct sentiment analysis in R, with an emphasis on practical applications and examples.

1. Text Mining: An Overview

Text mining refers to the process of deriving high-quality information from textual data. It encompasses various techniques and algorithms that facilitate the extraction of patterns, trends, and insights. At its core, text mining combines natural language processing (NLP), machine learning, and information retrieval.

1.1 Text Mining Process

The text mining process typically involves the following steps:

Data Collection: Gather textual data from various sources, such as social media, websites, or internal documents.

Preprocessing: Clean and preprocess the data to remove noise. This may involve removing stop words, punctuation, and performing lowercasing.

Tokenization: Split the text into smaller pieces (tokens), such as words or phrases, that can be analyzed.

Exploratory Data Analysis: Analyze the data to understand its structure and characteristics.

Feature Extraction: Convert the text into a numerical format that can be used for machine learning algorithms.

Modeling: Apply machine learning models to extract insights or make predictions.

Visualization: Present the findings through visualizations. ## 2. Tokenization: Breaking Down Text

121

Tokenization is a critical step in text mining that entails breaking down text into smaller units called tokens. Tokens can be words, phrases, or even sentences. This process allows for easier analysis and manipulation of text data.

2.1 Types of Tokenization

Word Tokenization: Separates text into individual words.

Sentence Tokenization: Divides text into sentences.

Subword Tokenization: Breaks words into smaller meaningful components, which can be useful in handling rare words or morphological variations.

2.2 Tokenization in R

In R, we can utilize various packages to perform tokenization. The `tidytext` package is one of the most popular libraries for text mining and provides an easy way to convert text data into tokens.

Example of Tokenization in R

```R
# Load required packages library(tidyverse)
library(tidytext)

# Sample text

text_data <- data.frame(text = c("Natural Language Processing is fascinating.", "R is a great tool for data analysis."))

# Tokenization
```

```
tokenized_data <- text_data %>% unnest_tokens(word,
text)

print(tokenized_data)
```

This code snippet demonstrates how to tokenize a simple dataset into individual words. ## 3. Sentiment Analysis: Understanding Emotion

Sentiment analysis is the computational task of determining the emotional tone behind a series of words. This technique is widely used in understanding public opinion, customer feedback, or social media sentiment.

3.1 Approaches to Sentiment Analysis

Lexicon-Based Approach: This method utilizes a predefined dictionary of words associated with sentiment scores.

Machine Learning Approach: This model-based method trains algorithms on labeled datasets to categorize sentiment.

3.2 Performing Sentiment Analysis in R

The `tidytext` package also provides functionalities for sentiment analysis. We can use sentiment lexicons such as Bing, AFINN, and NRC to calculate sentiment scores.

Example of Sentiment Analysis in R

```R
# Load required packages library(tidytext) library(dplyr)

# Sample text data

text_data <- data_frame(line = 1:4,
```

```
text = c("I love programming in R!", "Text mining can be
challenging.", "I hate bugs in code.",
```

"R is a powerful language."))

Tokenization

tidy_text <- text_data %>%

unnest_tokens(word, text)

Sentiment analysis using Bing lexicon sentiment_scores
<- tidy_text %>% inner_join(get_sentiments("bing"))
%>% count(line, sentiment)

print(sentiment_scores)
```
```

In this example, we tokenize the text and then join it with
the Bing sentiment lexicon to count positive and negative
sentiments.

4. Visualizing Sentiment Analysis Results

Visualizations play a crucial role in understanding
sentiment trends and patterns. R offers several packages,
including `ggplot2`, for creating informative
visualizations.

Example of Visualization in R

```R library(ggplot2)
```

Plot sentiment scores

```
ggplot(sentiment_scores, aes(x = factor(line), fill =
sentiment)) + geom_bar(position = "stack") +
```

labs(title = "Sentiment Analysis Results", x = "Text Line",

y = "Count",

```
fill               =               "Sentiment")              +
scale_fill_manual(values=c("negative"="red",
"positive"="blue")) + theme_minimal()
```
```

This code illustrates how to visualize the sentiment analysis results, providing a clear representation of positive and negative sentiments across text lines.

Text mining, tokenization, and sentiment analysis in R are powerful techniques for harnessing the insights hidden within textual data. Mastering these skills allows analysts and data scientists to turn unstructured text into structured data points, which can be used for building AI models that enhance decision-making processes.

## Building NLP Models Using tidytext and text2vec

By leveraging computational methods, NLP enables machines to understand, interpret, and generate human language in a way that is both meaningful and functional. As the demand for intelligent systems increases, the importance of building robust NLP models has never been greater.

In this chapter, we will explore how to build NLP models using the `tidytext` and `text2vec` packages in R. We will go through preprocessing text data, vectorizing the text, and building a simple prediction model. By utilizing a tidy approach to text analysis and efficient vectorization techniques, we will streamline the NLP workflow and prepare data for machine learning applications.

## Setting Up the Environment
```

Before we dive into model building, ensure you have the necessary packages installed. If you haven't installed `tidytext` and `text2vec`, you can do so by running the following commands in your R console:

```R
install.packages("tidytext")
install.packages("text2vec") install.packages("dplyr")
install.packages("ggplot2") # Optional for visualization
```

Data Preparation

To illustrate our NLP model-building process, we will use a sample dataset. Let's use the famous `sentiments` dataset from the `tidytext` package, which contains a list of words and their corresponding sentiment scores. We will also create a small sample text data frame for training our model.

```R
library(tidytext) library(dplyr)
# Load example data data("sentiments")
sample_data <- data.frame(text = c("I love programming.",
"This is terrible.",
"I am so happy with my results!", "I hate waiting in line."))
# Display the sample data print(sample_data)
```

Text Preprocessing

NLP tasks often involve substantial text cleaning and preprocessing. This includes tokenization, removing stop words, and perhaps stemming or lemmatization. The `tidytext` package helps streamline this process.

Tokenization and Cleaning

Tokenization is the process of splitting text into individual terms. In this example, we will clean the text and convert it to a tidy format.

```R
# Tokenization

tidy_text <- sample_data %>% unnest_tokens(word, text) %>% anti_join(stop_words) # Remove stop words

# Display tidy text print(tidy_text)
```

Vectorization with text2vec

Once we have our text data in a tidy format, we need to convert it into a structure that machine learning models can understand—numerical vectors. The `text2vec` package provides efficient tools for vectorization.

Creating Document-Term Matrix

We'll create a Document-Term Matrix (DTM) using `text2vec`. This matrix will contain the frequency of words across different documents (in our case, sentences).

```R library(text2vec)
# Prepare vocabulary

it <- itoken(tidy_text$word, progress_callback = function(x) x / length(tidy_text$word))

# Create vocabulary
```

```
vocab_vector <- create_vocabulary(it)
# Create vectorizer
vectorizer <- vocab_vector %>% vocab_vectorizer()
# Create DTM
dtm <- create_dtm(it, vectorizer)
# Display DTM print(dtm)
```

Building an NLP Model

With our DTM ready, we can now build a simple classification model. For demonstration, we will create a naive Bayes model to predict sentiment based on our sample sentences. Typically, for a real-world application, you'd have a labeled dataset for supervised learning.

Training the Model

Let's assume we have sentiment labels for our sample sentences. We'll create a simple mapping from the sample data to sentiments: "positive" or "negative".

```R
# Adding sentiment labels
sample_data$sentiment <- c("positive", "negative", "positive", "negative")
# Train a naive Bayes model using e1071 library
library(e1071)
# Train the model
model <- naiveBayes(as.factor(sentiment) ~ ., data =
```

as.data.frame(as.matrix(dtm)))

Check the model summary summary(model)

```

### Making Predictions

Now that we have our model trained, we can use it to make predictions on new text data.

```R

# New sentences for prediction

new_text <- data.frame(text = c("I dislike this product.", "Fantastic experience!"))

# Preprocess new text tidy_new <- new_text %>%

unnest_tokens(word, text) %>% anti_join(stop_words)

# Create DTM for new text it_new <- itoken(tidy_new$word)

dtm_new <- create_dtm(it_new, vectorizer)

# Make predictions

predictions <- predict(model, as.data.frame(as.matrix(dtm_new))) print(predictions)

```

Visualization and Evaluation

After model training and predictions, evaluating the model's performance is critical. We'll visualize the confusion matrix and review performance metrics such as accuracy.

```R

```
Create confusion matrix

confusion_matrix <- table(predictions, actual_labels)
print(confusion_matrix)

Visualize with ggplot2 library(ggplot2)

# Convert confusion matrix to data frame for plotting
confusion_df <- as.data.frame(confusion_matrix)

Plot confusion matrix

ggplot(confusion_df, aes(x = predictions, y = actual_labels)) +

geom_tile(aes(fill = Frequency), color = "white") +
scale_fill_gradient(low = "white", high = "blue") +

labs(title = "Confusion Matrix", x = "Predicted", y = "Actual")
```

We explored the process of building NLP models using the `tidytext` and `text2vec` packages in R. We covered preprocessing, vectorization, model training using naive Bayes, and making predictions. While our example was a simple demonstration, the techniques introduced here are foundational for more complex NLP tasks in real-world applications.

Chapter 9: Computer Vision with R

This chapter explores the tools and techniques available in R for implementing computer vision tasks, such as image recognition, object detection, and image segmentation.

Understanding Computer Vision

At its core, computer vision aims to replicate how humans use their visual systems to gain information about their surroundings. This involves multiple processes:

Image Processing: The manipulation of an image to enhance it or extract information. This may involve filtering, transforming, and analyzing the image data.

Feature Extraction: Identifying and isolating various features within an image, such as edges, colors, and textures, which can be used for further analysis.

Classification: Assigning labels to images based on their content using machine learning models.

The application of these processes can be seen in various domains—healthcare (e.g., medical imaging), autonomous vehicles (e.g., obstacle detection), and entertainment (e.g., facial recognition in photos).

Setting Up R for Computer Vision

Before diving into computer vision techniques, we need to set up our R environment. R provides several packages for image processing and analysis, with the most notable being:

magick: A powerful library for image processing that provides a wide range of functionalities, including reading, writing, and modifying images.

131

OpenCV: An interface to the popular OpenCV library, which is widely used for real-time computer vision tasks.

imager: A package for image analysis in R that supports basic image processing and mathematical operations on images.

Installation

You can install these packages from CRAN or GitHub. Here's how to get started:

```r
# Install required packages from CRAN
install.packages(c("magick", "imager"))

# Install OpenCV package from GitHub
if (!requireNamespace("devtools", quietly = TRUE)) {
install.packages("devtools")
}
devtools::install_github("surjik/imager")
```

Basic Image Processing with magick

Let's begin with some basic image operations using the `magick` package. This package simplifies the process of manipulating images with a coherent and user-friendly syntax.

Loading and Displaying Images

To load and display an image in R, we can use the `image_read` and `print` functions.

```r
```r library(magick)
# Load an image
img <- image_read("path/to/your/image.jpg")
# Display the image print(img)
```
```

Resizing and Cropping Images

Image manipulation often requires resizing and cropping. Here's how you can perform these operations:

```r
```r
# Resize the image to a width of 400 pixels while maintaining aspect ratio img_resized <- image_scale(img, "400")
# Crop the image to a specific region
img_cropped <- image_crop(img, "200x200+50+50")
# Display the modified images print(img_resized) print(img_cropped)
```
```

Applying Filters and Effects

To enhance images, you can apply various filters. The `magick` package offers a range of options.

```r
```r
# Apply a blur effect
img_blurred <- image_blur(img, radius = 5)
# Convert to grayscale
img_gray <- image_convert(img, colorspace = "Gray")
```
```

Display the effects print(img_blurred) print(img_gray)

```
```

Image Classification with Deep Learning

A critical application of computer vision is image classification, often solved using deep learning techniques. The `keras` and `tensorflow` packages in R provide interfaces to implement and train neural networks.

Setting Up the Keras Environment

Before building a model, you need to install Keras and TensorFlow.

```r
install.packages("keras") library(keras)
```

Install TensorFlow library(tensorflow) install_tensorflow()

```
```

Building a Convolutional Neural Network (CNN)

Convolutional Neural Networks (CNNs) are particularly effective for image classification tasks. Here's a basic example of building a CNN in R:

```r
```

Load libraries library(keras)

Load the dataset (e.g., CIFAR-10) cifar10 <- dataset_cifar10()

Preprocess the data

x_train <- cifar10$train$x / 255

y_train <- to_categorical(cifar10$train$y, num_classes =

10)

```r
# Define the CNN model
model <- keras_model_sequential() %>%
layer_conv_2d(filters = 32, kernel_size = c(3, 3),
activation = 'relu', input_shape = c(32, 32, 3)) %>%
layer_max_pooling_2d(pool_size = c(2, 2)) %>%

layer_conv_2d(filters = 64, kernel_size = c(3, 3),
activation = 'relu') %>%
layer_max_pooling_2d(pool_size = c(2, 2)) %>%

layer_flatten() %>%

layer_dense(units = 128, activation = 'relu') %>%
layer_dense(units = 10, activation = 'softmax')

# Compile the model
model %>% compile(loss = 'categorical_crossentropy',
optimizer = 'adam', metrics = c('accuracy'))

# Train the model
model %>% fit(x_train, y_train, epochs = 10, batch_size
= 64, validation_split = 0.2)
```

Evaluating Model Performance

Once you've trained the model, evaluating its performance on a separate test set is crucial.

```r
# Load the test data
cifar10_test <- dataset_cifar10()$test x_test <-
cifar10_test$x / 255
```

```
y_test <- to_categorical(cifar10_test$y, num_classes =
10)
```

Evaluate the model

```
scores <- model %>% evaluate(x_test, y_test)

cat('Test loss:', scores[1]) cat('Test accuracy:', scores[2])
```
```

## Image Segmentation using OpenCV

In addition to classification, image segmentation is another pivotal computer vision task. It involves partitioning an image into multiple segments to simplify analysis. Using the `OpenCV` interface in R, we can achieve effective segmentation.

### Basic Image Segmentation

Here's a simple example of using color-based segmentation with OpenCV:

```r
library(OpenCV)
```

Read the image

```
img_opencv <- imread("path/to/your/image.jpg")
```

Convert the image to HSV color space

```
hsv <- cvtColor(img_opencv, COLOR_BGR2HSV)
```

Define the range for the color you want to segment (e.g., blue) lower_blue <- c(100, 100, 100)

```
upper_blue <- c(140, 255, 255)
```

Create a mask for the blue color

```
mask <- inRange(hsv, lower_blue, upper_blue)
```
```

Apply the mask to get the segmented image

segmented <- bitwise_and(img_opencv, img_opencv, mask = mask)

Display the segmented image imshow("Segmented Image", segmented) waitKey(0) # Wait for a key press
```

### Advanced Techniques

The field of image segmentation also includes advanced techniques such as using U-Net architectures for semantic segmentation. These techniques can be implemented in R similarly to CNNs, allowing for powerful and precise segmentation of images.

We explored the fundamentals of computer vision with R for AI applications, including basic image processing techniques, deep learning for image classification, and segmentation techniques using OpenCV. The combination of R's statistical prowess and advanced machine learning techniques provides a robust foundation for computer vision applications.

# Image Processing with imager and magick

This chapter delves into the functionalities offered by these packages and demonstrates how to leverage them for AI-related tasks.

## 1. Overview of imager and magick ### 1.1 imager

The **imager** package provides a comprehensive framework for image processing in R. Designed with a focus on efficiency and high performance, it allows users
```

to perform a variety of tasks, including:

Image reading and writing

Image manipulation (resizing, rotating, flipping)

Filtering and convolution

Feature detection

Color manipulation

Image segmentation

Installation:

To use the `imager` package, install it from CRAN using the following command:

```R
install.packages("imager")
```

1.2 magick

magick is an R wrapper around the ImageMagick library, known for its vast capabilities in handling images. It excels in:

Image resizing and cropping

Filters and effects

Drawing and annotations

Animation creation

Compositing multiple images

Installation:

To install the `magick` package, use:

```R
install.packages("magick")
```

```
```

2. Basic Image Operations

2.1 Reading and Displaying Images

To start working with images, you must first load them into R. Using both packages, reading and displaying images is straightforward.

Using imager:

```R
library(imager)
# Read an image
img <- load.image("path/to/image.jpg")
# Display the image plot(img)
```

Using magick:

```R
library(magick)
# Read an image
img_magick <- image_read("path/to/image.jpg")
# Display the image print(img_magick)
```

2.2 Image Resizing and Cropping

Resizing and cropping images is a common operation in preprocessing for AI models.

With imager:

```R
```

```R
# Resize the image to 100x100 pixels img_resized <-
resize(img, 100, 100) plot(img_resized)
```

With magick:

```R
# Resize the image

img_resized_magick <- image_resize(img_magick,
"100x100") print(img_resized_magick)
```

2.3 Image Filtering

Filters enhance images by modifying their pixel values,
which can be critical for feature extraction in AI models.

Applying filters with imager:

```R
# Apply a Gaussian blur

img_blur <- isoblur(img, sigma = 2) plot(img_blur)


```

Applying filters with magick:

```R
# Apply a Gaussian blur

img_blur_magick <- image_blur(img_magick, radius = 5,
sigma = 3) print(img_blur_magick)
```

3. Advanced Image Processing Techniques ### 3.1 Edge Detection

Edge detection is crucial for many computer vision tasks. Both packages offer methods for this.

Using imager's Canny edge detector:

```R
img_edges <- imgradient(img, "xy") plot(img_edges)
```

Using magick's edge detection:

```R
img_edges_magick    <-    image_edges(img_magick)
print(img_edges_magick)
```

3.2 Color Manipulation

Manipulating colors can be particularly useful in image processing for feature enhancement or image segmentation.

Using imager to change brightness:

```R
# Increase brightness img_bright <- img * 1.2
plot(img_bright)
```

Using magick for color adjustments:

```R
# Change color saturation
```

```
img_saturated    <-    image_modulate(img_magick,
brightness = 120, saturation = 150) print(img_saturated)
```

4. Preparing Images for AI Models

Making images ready for input into AI models typically
involves resizing, normalization, and augmentation.

4.1 Normalization

Normalizing images ensures uniformity for model
training.

```R
# Normalize values between 0 and 1 for imager images
img_normalized <- img / 255
```

4.2 Image Augmentation

Augmenting images artificially increases the dataset size,
improving model robustness.

1. Using imager:

```R
# Randomly flipping images img_flipped <- imflip(img)
```

2. Using magick:

```R
# Rotate the image by 45 degrees
img_rotated    <-    image_rotate(img_magick,    45)
```

```
print(img_rotated)
```

5. Case Study: Applying Image Processing for CNN

In this section, we will apply the learned techniques to prepare images for a Convolutional Neural Network (CNN).

Step 1: Load and Preprocess Images

Load images from a dataset, resize, normalize and augment them as necessary.

```R
# Load images from a directory and preprocess

images <- list.files("path/to/data", pattern = "*.jpg", full.names = TRUE) image_list <- lapply(images, function(x) {

img <- load.image(x)

img <- resize(img, 100, 100) img <- img / 255 # Normalize return(img)

})
```

Step 2: Train a Simple CNN

Utilizing the preprocessed images, we can feed them into a simple CNN model using Keras.

```R
library(keras)

model <- keras_model_sequential() %>%
```

```
layer_conv_2d(filters = 32, kernel_size = c(3, 3),
activation = 'relu', input_shape = c(100, 100, 3)) %>%
layer_max_pooling_2d(pool_size = c(2, 2)) %>%

layer_flatten() %>%

layer_dense(units = 128, activation = 'relu') %>%
layer_dense(units = 10, activation = 'softmax')


model %>% compile(loss = 'categorical_crossentropy',
optimizer = 'adam', metrics = c('accuracy'))
```

Step 3: Training the Model

Fit the model using the training data.

```R
history <- model %>% fit(x = image_list, y = labels,
epochs = 10, validation_split = 0.2)
```

With a foundation in basic image manipulation, users can explore more complex tasks, maintain high-quality datasets, and improve the performance of their AI models. By harnessing the power of these packages, you'll be well-equipped to handle diverse image-related challenges in your analytical projects.

Deep Learning for Image Classification with keras

In this chapter, we will explore the powerful capabilities of Keras, a high-level deep learning library that allows for the rapid development and experimentation of neural networks. We will focus on image classification tasks using Keras in R and provide a step-by-step guide to building effective models that can categorize images into predefined classes.

Understanding Image Classification

Image classification is a fundamental problem in computer vision, where the objective is to assign a label to an input image based on its visual content. Typical applications of image classification include:

Facial recognition: Identifying individuals from photographs.

Object detection: Identifying and locating objects within images.

Medical image analysis: Classifying images of tissues or organs to assist in diagnostics.

The classification task typically involves training a model on a labeled dataset, where each image has a corresponding label. Once trained, the model can predict the labels of unseen images.

Setting Up the Environment

Before diving into the implementation, ensure that you have R and the necessary libraries installed. You can install Keras in R using the following commands:

```R
install.packages("keras")
library(keras)
install_keras()
```

This command will also install TensorFlow, which is the backend for Keras. Make sure that you are connected to the internet as it may take some time to download the necessary packages.

Loading and Preprocessing Data

For our image classification task, we'll use a popular dataset called CIFAR-10, which consists of 60,000 32x32 color images in 10 classes, with 6,000 images per class. The classes are:

Airplane

Automobile

Bird

Cat

Deer

Dog

Frog

Horse

Ship

Truck

Loading the Data

We can easily load the CIFAR-10 dataset using Keras:

```R
# Load the dataset

cifar10    <-    dataset_cifar10()    train_images    <-
cifar10$train$x    train_labels    <-    cifar10$train$y
test_images    <-    cifar10$test$x    test_labels    <-
```

cifar10$test$y
```

### Preprocessing

Preprocessing is vital for model performance. We will normalize the pixel values to be between 0 and 1 and convert the labels to a categorical format:

```R

# Normalize pixel values train_images <- train_images / 255 test_images <- test_images / 255

# Convert labels to categorical format train_labels <- to_categorical(train_labels, 10) test_labels <- to_categorical(test_labels, 10)
```

Building the Model

Now we are ready to build our convolutional neural network (CNN) model. CNNs are especially effective for image analysis tasks due to their ability to capture spatial hierarchies in images.

Model Architecture

We will create a simple CNN architecture composed of convolutional layers, max-pooling layers, and dense layers:

```R

model <- keras_model_sequential() %>%

layer_conv_2d(filters = 32, kernel_size = c(3, 3), activation = 'relu', input_shape = c(32, 32, 3)) %>% layer_max_pooling_2d(pool_size = c(2, 2)) %>%
```
```

```
layer_conv_2d(filters = 64, kernel_size = c(3, 3),
activation                =                'relu')        %>%
layer_max_pooling_2d(pool_size = c(2, 2)) %>%

layer_flatten() %>%

layer_dense(units = 64, activation = 'relu') %>%
layer_dense(units = 10, activation = 'softmax')
```

Compiling the Model

After defining the model architecture, we need to compile it by specifying the optimizer, loss function, and evaluation metric:

```R
model %>% compile(


loss = 'categorical_crossentropy', optimizer = optimizer_adam(), metrics = c('accuracy')
)
```

Training the Model

With the model compiled, we can proceed to train it using the training dataset. We'll fit the model for a specified number of epochs and define the batch size:

```R
history <- model %>% fit( train_images, train_labels, epochs = 10,

batch_size = 64,
```

validation_split = 0.2

)
```

### Monitoring Training

To track the performance of the model during training, we can utilize the `history` object, which contains loss and accuracy information. We can visualize the training progress using plots:

```R library(ggplot2)

# Plot training & validation accuracy values

plot(history$metrics$accuracy, type = "l", col = "blue", xlab = "Epoch", ylab = "Accuracy") lines(history$metrics$val_accuracy, col = "red")

legend("topright", legend = c("Training", "Validation"), col = c("blue", "red"), lty = 1)
```

Evaluating the Model

After training the model, it's essential to evaluate its performance on the test dataset to understand how well it generalizes to unseen data:

```R

test_loss, test_acc <- model %>% evaluate(test_images, test_labels) print(paste("Test Accuracy:", test_acc))
```

Making Predictions

With the model trained and evaluated, we can use it to

149
```

make predictions on new images:

```R
predictions <- model %>% predict(test_images)

# Get the class with the highest probability
predicted_classes <- apply(predictions, 1, which.max)
```

We walked through the process of developing an image classification model using deep learning in R with Keras. We discussed the foundational concepts of image classification, the importance of preprocessing, and how to build, compile, and train a convolutional neural network.

Chapter 10: Time Series Forecasting Using AI

In this chapter, we will delve into the exciting world of time series forecasting using Artificial Intelligence (AI) within the R programming ecosystem. R is widely recognized for its powerful statistical capabilities, and when combined with AI techniques, it becomes an effective tool for making predictions based on past observations.

10.1 Understanding Time Series Data ### 10.1.1 What is Time Series Data?

Time series data is a sequence of observations recorded at specific time intervals. Examples include daily stock prices, monthly sales figures, or yearly temperature readings. The dataset's temporal ordering is crucial, as it reflects the underlying patterns influenced by time.

10.1.2 Key Components of Time Series Data

Trend: The long-term movement in the data, indicating whether it is increasing, decreasing, or remaining stationary over time.

Seasonality: Regular repeating fluctuations that occur at specific intervals, such as hourly, daily, monthly, or yearly.

Cyclic Patterns: These are long-term fluctuations that do not have a fixed period, often related to economic or environmental factors.

Noise: Random variations that cannot be attributed to trend, seasonality, or cycles. Understanding these components helps in selecting the right forecasting model.

10.2 Preparing Time Series Data in R

Before performing AI-driven forecasting, it's essential to preprocess the time series data. ### 10.2.1 Importing Libraries

We will need a few libraries to facilitate our analysis. The key libraries include `forecast`, `tidyverse`,

`tsibble`, and machine learning packages like `caret` or `keras` for deep learning models.

```R
# Install necessary packages if not already installed
install.packages(c("forecast", "tidyverse", "tsibble", "caret","keras"))

# Load libraries library(forecast) library(tidyverse) library(tsibble) library(caret) library(keras)
```

10.2.2 Loading and Exploring the Data

Assume we have a dataset containing historical sales data. We'll load this data and perform some exploratory data analysis (EDA).

```R
# Load dataset

data <- read.csv("sales_data.csv", stringsAsFactors = FALSE)

# Convert to time series object

ts_data <- ts(data$sales, start = c(2015, 1), frequency = 12)
```

```
# Plotting the time series data
plot(ts_data, main = "Sales Data Over Time", ylab =
"Sales", xlab = "Year")
```

10.2.3 Decomposing Time Series

We can decompose the time series to better understand its components.

```R
decomposed_data        <-        decompose(ts_data)
plot(decomposed_data)
```

10.3 Traditional Forecasting Techniques

While AI methods are promising, it's crucial to understand traditional forecasting techniques, such as ARIMA and Exponential Smoothing, as a baseline.

10.3.1 ARIMA (AutoRegressive Integrated Moving Average)

ARIMA is a widely-used statistical method for time series forecasting that captures dependencies in historical data.

```R
# Fit ARIMA model
fit <- auto.arima(ts_data) summary(fit)

# Forccasting
forecasted_values    <-    forecast(fit,    h    =    12)
plot(forecasted_values)
```

10.3.2 Exponential Smoothing State Space Model (ETS)

Another traditional approach is the ETS model, suitable for capturing trends and seasonality effectively.

```R
# Fit ETS model fit_ets <- ets(ts_data) summary(fit_ets)
# Forecasting
forecast_ets <- forecast(fit_ets, h = 12) plot(forecast_ets)


```

10.4 AI-Driven Forecasting Techniques

While the traditional methods are valuable, AI techniques have shown remarkable capabilities in leveraging vast amounts of data and complex relationships.

10.4.1 Neural Networks and LSTM

Neural networks, specifically Long Short-Term Memory (LSTM) networks, are excellent for capturing sequential dependencies in time series data.

Data Preparation for LSTM

To apply LSTM, we typically reshape our data into a format suitable for training the neural network.

```R
# Data normalization and splitting library(caret)
normalized_data <- scale(ts_data)
train_data                                          <-
normalized_data[1:(length(normalized_data) - 12)]
```

154

```R
test_data <- normalized_data[(length(normalized_data) -
11):length(normalized_data)]
# Reshape to [samples, time steps, features]
train_array        <-        array(train_data,        dim        =
c(length(train_data), 1, 1))
```

Building the LSTM Model

```R
# Define the LSTM model
model <- keras_model_sequential() %>%
layer_lstm(units = 50, activation = 'relu', input_shape =
c(1, 1)) %>% layer_dense(units = 1)
# Compile the model
model %>% compile(loss = 'mean_squared_error',
optimizer = 'adam')
# Fit the model
model %>% fit(train_array, train_data, epochs = 100,
batch_size = 16, verbose = 1)
```

Making Predictions

Once the model is trained, we can forecast future values.

```R
# Prepare test data
test_array <- array(test_data, dim = c(length(test_data),
1, 1))
```

```
# Predict
predictions <- model %>% predict(test_array)
```

10.4.2 Hybrid Models

Hybrid models that combine traditional methods with AI techniques often yield robust results, capturing different patterns in the data effectively.

10.5 Model Evaluation

After obtaining forecasts, evaluating the model is crucial to ensure its accuracy. ### 10.5.1 Metrics for Evaluation

Common metrics include Mean Absolute Error (MAE), Mean Squared Error (MSE), and Root Mean Squared Error (RMSE).

```R
# Calculate metrics
mae <- mean(abs(test_data - predictions)) mse <- mean((test_data - predictions)^2) rmse <- sqrt(mse)
cat("MAE:", mae, "\nMSE:", mse, "\nRMSE:", rmse)
```

We explored time series forecasting using AI in R programming. We covered the preparation of data, traditional forecasting techniques such as ARIMA and ETS, as well as AI-driven approaches using neural networks, particularly LSTM models. Lastly, the importance of model evaluation was highlighted, providing a comprehensive understanding of the forecasting process.

Classical Time Series Techniques with forecast and tsibble

This chapter delves into classical time series techniques using the R programming language, particularly focusing on the `forecast` and `tsibble` packages. We will begin by establishing a foundational understanding of time series data, explore key classical methods, and illustrate how to implement these techniques using R.

Understanding Time Series Data

A time series is a sequence of data points collected or recorded at specific time intervals. Time series data can be categorized into different components:

Trend: The long-term movement in the data.

Seasonality: The repeating short-term cycle in the data, which occurs at regular intervals.

Noise: The random variation in the data that cannot be attributed to the trend or seasonal effects. ## The Importance of Forecasting

Forecasting refers to the process of predicting future values based on historical data. It is widely used in various fields such as finance, economics, weather forecasting, and inventory management. Classical time series techniques provide robust frameworks for generating forecasts. By leveraging R's `forecast` and

`tsibble` packages, we can efficiently handle and analyze time series data. ## Getting Started with R

Before embarking on time series analysis, ensure that R

and the necessary packages are installed. Use the following commands to install the packages:

```R
install.packages("forecast") install.packages("tsibble")
install.packages("fable")
```

Load the packages into your R environment:

```R
library(forecast) library(tsibble) library(fable)
```

Classifying Time Series Data

The first step in time series analysis is to class your data into a suitable format. The `tsibble` package serves as a powerful tool for representing and manipulating time series data. Consider this simple example using monthly sales data:

```R
# Sample Data Creation sales_data <- data.frame(
month = seq.Date(from = as.Date("2020-01-01"), by = "month", length.out = 24), sales = c(120, 135, 150, 180, 210, 230, 260, 300, 320, 360, 390, 400,
420, 460, 500, 550, 600, 640, 670, 700, 740, 800, 850, 900)
)
# Converting to tsibble
sales_tsibble <- as_tsibble(sales_data, index = month)
```

Exploring Classical Forecasting Techniques

1. Autoregressive Integrated Moving Average (ARIMA)

ARIMA models are a blend of autoregression (AR) and moving average (MA) concepts, along with the integration (I) of the series to make it stationary. A key strength of ARIMA is its ability to model a wide variety of time series data.

To fit an ARIMA model:

```R
# Fit ARIMA model

fit_arima <- sales_tsibble %>% model(ARIMA(sales))

# Review the model summary report(fit_arima)
```

2. Exponential Smoothing State Space Model (ETS)

ETS models utilize exponential smoothing techniques. They are particularly effective for capturing trend and seasonality without requiring a complex model specification.

To fit an ETS model:

```R
# Fit ETS model

fit_ets <- sales_tsibble %>% model(ETS(sales))

# Review model summary report(fit_ets)
```

3. Seasonal Decomposition of Time Series (STL)

159

Seasonal decomposition allows for the extraction of trend and seasonal components from a time series. This is essential for understanding the underlying structure of the data.

To visualize the decomposition:

```R
# Decomposing time series stl_decomp <- sales_tsibble %>% model(STL(sales))

# Plot the decomposition components(stl_decomp) %>% autoplot()
```

Making Forecasts

Once models are fitted, the next step is to generate forecasts. We can use the `forecast` function from the

`fable` package to generate future predictions.

```R
# Forecasting with ARIMA forecasts_arima <- fit_arima %>% forecast(h = "12 months")

# Plot ARIMA forecasts autoplot(forecasts_arima) + ggtitle("ARIMA Forecast for Sales Data")
```

Similar steps can be done for the ETS model or any other models:

```R
# Forecasting with ETS forecasts_ets <- fit_ets %>%
```

160

forecast(h = "12 months")

Plot ETS forecasts autoplot(forecasts_ets) +

ggtitle("ETS Forecast for Sales Data")
``` ` ` `

Model Evaluation

To evaluate the performance of our forecasting models, we can use common accuracy metrics like Mean Absolute Percentage Error (MAPE) or Root Mean Squared Error (RMSE).

```` ` ` `R

Evaluate model accuracy accuracy(forecasts_arima, sales_monthly_test)   accuracy(forecasts_ets, sales_monthly_test)
``` ` ` `

We covered the classical time series techniques vital for making predictions. We utilized R's `forecast` and

`tsibble` packages to manipulate, analyze, and forecast time series data effectively. Understanding these concepts and their implementation can significantly enhance the predictive capabilities of AI applications across various domains.

Deep Learning Models for Sequential Data in R

This chapter explores various deep learning models specifically designed for handling sequential data, with a focus on how to implement these models in R.

Understanding Sequential Data
```

Sequential data is characterized by the fact that the order of the observations matters. For example, in a time series forecasting problem, the prediction for the next time step depends on the preceding values. Similarly, in natural language processing (NLP), the meaning of a word can depend heavily on the context provided by preceding and following words.

Common types of sequential data include:

Time series data (e.g., stock prices, weather data)

Text data (e.g., sentences, documents)

Audio data (e.g., speech signals)

Biological sequences (e.g., DNA sequencing)

Given the unique properties of sequential data, specialized modeling techniques are often required to capture the temporal dependencies and structure inherent in the data.

Deep Learning Architectures for Sequential Data

Recurrent Neural Networks (RNNs)

RNNs are one of the most widely used architectures for sequential data. They are designed to leverage the sequential nature of the data by maintaining a hidden state that carries information from previous time steps. RNNs can be particularly effective for tasks like language modeling, text generation, and time series prediction.

Implementation in R

The `keras` package in R allows for the easy construction of RNNs. Below is a simple example of an RNN model for a time series forecasting problem:

```R
library(keras)
```

```r
# Prepare your data (X_train, y_train) in the required shape model <- keras_model_sequential() %>%

layer_lstm(units = 50, input_shape = c(timesteps, features)) %>% layer_dense(units = 1)

model %>% compile(loss = 'mean_squared_error', optimizer = 'adam') model %>% fit(X_train, y_train, epochs = 100, batch_size = 32)
```

Long Short-Term Memory Networks (LSTMs)

LSTMs are a special kind of RNN that are adept at learning long-term dependencies. They are particularly suited for sequence prediction tasks because they can effectively learn to remember information for long periods of time. This makes LSTMs a popular choice for applications in NLP and time series forecasting.

Implementation in R

The implementation of LSTMs in R follows a similar structure to RNNs, as demonstrated below:

```r
model <- keras_model_sequential() %>%

layer_lstm(units = 50, input_shape = c(timesteps, features), return_sequences = TRUE) %>% layer_lstm(units = 50) %>%

layer_dense(units = 1)

model %>% compile(loss = 'mean_squared_error', optimizer = 'adam') model %>% fit(X_train, y_train,
```

```
epochs = 100, batch_size = 32)
```
` ` `

Gated Recurrent Units (GRUs)

GRUs are similar to LSTMs but with a slightly simpler architecture. They combine the forget and input gates into a single update gate, which can lead to faster training times and similar performance for many tasks. GRUs are often preferred for applications where computational resources are limited.

Implementation in R

Implementing GRUs in R is straightforward, as shown in the following code snippet:

` ` `R

```
model <- keras_model_sequential() %>%

layer_gru(units = 50, input_shape = c(timesteps, features)) %>% layer_dense(units = 1)

model %>% compile(loss = 'mean_squared_error', optimizer = 'adam') model %>% fit(X_train, y_train, epochs = 100, batch_size = 32)
```
` ` `

Convolutional Neural Networks (CNNs) for Sequences

Although CNNs are typically associated with image data, they can also be adapted for sequential data. When treating the sequential data as a "1D image," convolutional layers can capture local patterns effectively. This approach can be particularly useful when modeling sequential data with fixed-size windows.

164

Implementation in R

Here's a simple CNN model for sequential data:

```R
model <- keras_model_sequential() %>%

layer_conv1d(filters = 32, kernel_size = 3, activation = 'relu', input_shape = c(timesteps, features)) %>%
layer_max_pooling1d(pool_size = 2) %>%

layer_flatten() %>%


layer_dense(units = 1)

model %>% compile(loss = 'mean_squared_error', optimizer = 'adam') model %>% fit(X_train, y_train, epochs = 100, batch_size = 32)
```

Summary and Best Practices

Deep learning models for sequential data can effectively capture complex patterns and dependencies inherent in the data. In R, packages such as `keras` provide powerful tools to construct and train various architectures like RNNs, LSTMs, GRUs, and CNNs.

Best Practices:

Experiment with different architectures to find the one that best captures the patterns in your specific dataset.

Tune hyperparameters such as learning rate, batch size, and number of epochs based on validation performance.

Use techniques like dropout and regularization to prevent

overfitting, especially in deep networks.

Make sure to preprocess your data appropriately, including normalization and windowing for time series.

By leveraging the power of deep learning, analysts and data scientists can open new avenues for insights in sequential data, paving the way for more informed decision-making and innovative applications across various industries.

Chapter 11: Explainable AI and Model Interpretability

This chapter delves into Explainable AI (XAI) and model interpretability, focusing on practical implementations using R, a popular programming language in data science.

11.1 The Importance of Explainable AI

Explainable AI refers to methods and techniques that make the workings of AI models understandable to humans. The significance of XAI is multifaceted:

Trust and Accountability: Users are more likely to trust AI systems if they can understand how decisions are made. This is crucial in areas such as healthcare, finance, and law, where the consequences of incorrect predictions can be severe.

Regulatory Compliance: Many jurisdictions are beginning to enforce regulations that require AI systems to be interpretable. The European Union's General Data Protection Regulation (GDPR) emphasizes the "right to explanation," making it vital for organizations to adopt XAI practices.

Model Improvement: Understanding how a model arrives at its decisions can expose weaknesses and biases, leading to improvements in model performance.

Collaborative Insights: Interpretability aids interdisciplinary collaboration, allowing data scientists to communicate their findings effectively to domain experts.

11.2 Model Interpretability Techniques ### 11.2.1 Global vs. Local Interpretability

Model interpretability techniques can be broadly categorized into global and local methods:

Global Interpretability provides an understanding of the overall model behavior. This can be achieved through techniques like feature importance and partial dependence plots.

Local Interpretability focuses on specific predictions. It helps decipher why a model made a particular prediction for a specific instance. Techniques such as Local Interpretable Model-agnostic Explanations (LIME) and Shapley Additive Explanations (SHAP) fall into this category.

11.2.2 Feature Importance

Feature importance techniques rank variables based on their contributions to the model's predictions. In R, one common method for calculating feature importance is through the use of Random Forests.

```r
# Install required packages install.packages("randomForest") library(randomForest)

# Load dataset data(iris)

# Fit model set.seed(123)

rf_model <- randomForest(Species ~ ., data = iris)

# Calculate feature importance

importance_df <- as.data.frame(importance(rf_model)) importance_df$features <- rownames(importance_df)

# Plot feature importance library(ggplot2)
```

```r
ggplot(importance_df, aes(x=reorder(features, MeanDecreaseGini), y=MeanDecreaseGini)) +
geom_bar(stat="identity", fill="steelblue") +

coord_flip() +

labs(title="Feature Importance", x="Features", y="Mean Decrease in Gini Index")
```

11.2.3 LIME

LIME provides local explanations for individual predictions. Imagine explaining why a customer was flagged for loan rejection. Here's how to implement LIME in R.

```r
# Install required packages install.packages("lime")
library(lime)

# Prepare data

explainer <- lime(iris[-5], model = rf_model)

# Explain prediction for an instance

explanation <- explain(iris[1, -5, drop = FALSE], explainer,

n_labels = 1,

n_features = 2)

# Plot explanation plot_features(explanation)
```

11.2.4 SHAP

SHAP values provide a unified measure of feature

importance. In R, the `shapr` package can be utilized to compute SHAP values.

```r
# Install required packages install.packages("shapr")
library(shapr)

# Prepare data X_train <- iris[,-5]

explainer <- shapr(X_train, rf_model)


# Compute SHAP values for a specific instance X_new <-
iris[1, -5, drop = FALSE]

shap_values <- explain(X_new, explainer, n_samples =
1000)

# Visualize SHAP values library(ggplot2)

ggplot(shap_values, aes(x = Feature, y = value)) +
geom_bar(stat = "identity") +

labs(title = "SHAP Values for Instance", x = "Features", y
= "SHAP Value")

```

11.3 Challenges of Explainable AI

While explainable AI brings significant benefits, it also presents challenges:

Trade-off Between Accuracy and Interpretability: More complex models like deep learning can yield high accuracy but often lack interpretability.

Model Misinterpretation: Users may misinterpret explanations, especially when lacking domain knowledge.

Computational Complexity: Some explainability methods can be computationally intensive, particularly for large datasets.

Evolving Algorithms: As AI continues to evolve, keeping up with explainability methods that suit new algorithms can be challenging.

11.4 Conclusion

Explainable AI is essential for harnessing the full potential of AI technologies while ensuring ethical use. R provides robust tools and methodologies for building interpretable models and communicating the workings behind AI systems effectively. By incorporating explainability into AI processes, stakeholders can make informed decisions that align with ethical standards and societal norms.

As you continue your journey in AI development, keep the principles of explainability at the forefront. The ability to elucidate model behavior is not merely a technical skill but a crucial component of responsible AI practice.

This chapter serves as an introductory guide to explainable AI in the context of R, illustrating both its importance and practical applications. You are now equipped to implement these techniques and further explore the dimensions of model interpretability in your own AI journeys.

SHAP, LIME, and DALEX for Understanding AI Models

In this chapter, we will explore three powerful tools in the R programming environment: SHAP (SHapley Additive exPlanations), LIME (Local Interpretable Model-agnostic Explanations), and DALEX (Descriptive mAchine Learning EXplanations). Each of these methodologies provides unique perspectives and functionalities for explaining AI models, empowering users to build trust and transparency in their predictive analytics.

Understanding the Need for Model Interpretability

Before delving into the specific tools, it's essential to understand why model interpretability is critical. As machine learning models become more sophisticated, particularly with the rise of deep learning and ensemble methods, they often resemble "black boxes," making it difficult for users to understand the reasoning behind predictions.

Interpretability is fundamental for several reasons:

Trust: Stakeholders need to trust the models to make informed decisions.

Compliance: Many industries are subject to regulatory requirements that mandate transparency in decision-making processes.

Debugging: Understanding model predictions can help identify flaws in the data, model, or both.

Feature Importance: Knowing which features contribute most to predictions can guide further data collection and feature engineering.

Now, let's delve into our three primary tools, exploring their concepts, strengths, and how to implement them in R.

SHAP: SHapley Additive exPlanations ### Concept

SHAP values are based on cooperative game theory and provide a unified measure of feature importance. The fundamental idea is to allocate the "payout" (model prediction) fairly to the features (players) that contributed to the prediction. SHAP allows us to explain the output of any machine learning model by providing a global and local feature importance suite.

Implementation in R

To use SHAP in R, we'll employ the `shap` and `fastshap` packages. Let's consider a simple example using a random forest model on the built-in Iris dataset:

```r
# Install necessary packages
install.packages("randomForest")
install.packages("fastshap")        library(randomForest)
library(fastshap)


# Load the data data(iris)

# Train a random forest model set.seed(42)

rf_model <- randomForest(Species ~ ., data = iris, importance = TRUE)

# Use fastshap for SHAP value calculation

shap_values <- fastshap::fastshap(rf_model, X = iris[,-5], pred_wrapper = function(object, newdata) predict(object, newdata, type = "prob"))

# Visualize SHAP values library(ggplot2)

shap_df <- data.frame(SHAP = unlist(shap_values), Feature = rep(names(iris)[-5], nrow(iris)))
```

```r
ggplot(shap_df, aes(x = Feature, y = SHAP)) +
geom_boxplot() + theme_minimal() + labs(title = "SHAP
Values for Features in Iris Dataset")
```

This code snippet trains a random forest model on the Iris
dataset and calculates the SHAP values for each feature.
The visualization helps us understand the influence of
each feature on model predictions.

LIME: Local Interpretable Model-agnostic
Explanations ### Concept

LIME offers a different angle, focusing on the local
interpretability of model predictions. Instead of providing
a comprehensive view of feature importance, LIME
interprets the predictions of complex models by
approximating them with simple linear models in the
vicinity of the prediction. This makes it suitable for
understanding individual predictions.

Implementation in R

To use LIME, we can utilize the `lime` package in R.
Continuing with the Iris dataset, let's interpret a specific
prediction:

```r
# Install necessary package install.packages("lime")
library(lime)

# Create a function for prediction predict_fn <-
function(model, newdata) {

predict(model, newdata, type = "prob")[, "setosa"] #
Probability of being 'setosa'
```

```
}
```
Apply LIME

```
explainer <- lime(iris[-5], model = rf_model)
lime_results <- explain(iris[1:5, -5], explainer, n_labels =
1, n_features = 2)
```

Plot the LIME explanation plot_features(lime_results)
```
```

In this example, we use LIME to explain the predictions for a few samples in the Iris dataset. The visual output illustrates the contribution of each feature to specific predictions, providing insight into how the model arrived at its conclusions.

DALEX: Descriptive mAchine Learning EXplanations
Concept

DALEX provides a comprehensive toolbox for understanding and interpreting machine learning models. Unlike SHAP and LIME, which focus on individual predictions, DALEX supports both local and global interpretability through a cohesive suite of visualization tools and diagnostic metrics for model evaluation.

Implementation in R

To implement DALEX, we will use its rich ecosystem to compare models and visualize their behaviors:

```r
# Install necessary packages install.packages("DALEX")
library(DALEX)
```

Create an explainer object

```
explainer <- explain(rf_model, data = iris[-5], y =
iris$Species)
```

Model performance

```
model_performance <- model_performance(explainer)
```

\# Visualize the model performance
```
plot(model_performance)
```

Feature importance

```
feature_importance <- feature_importance(explainer)
plot(feature_importance)
```
```
` ` `
```

This snippet demonstrates how to articulate model behavior and evaluate the performance of the random forest model using DALEX's explaining functions. The resulting plots provide invaluable insights into model accuracy and feature contribution, fostering a deeper understanding of the model.

We explored SHAP, LIME, and DALEX—three robust tools in R that facilitate our understanding of AI models. Each framework brings unique advantages, and the choice of tool often depends on the specific requirements for interpretability—whether global insights or local explanations are desired.

Creating Visual AI Dashboards with flexdashboard and plotly

The rise of Artificial Intelligence (AI) and machine learning has made it necessary to communicate complex findings simply and intuitively. R, a powerful language for statistical computing and graphics, offers excellent packages to create interactive dashboards. In this chapter, we will explore how to create visually appealing dashboards using **flexdashboard** and **plotly** in R.

We will walk you through the process step-by-step, enabling you to transform data into interactive visualizations that enhance your analysis of AI-generated results.

Setting Up Your R Environment

Before diving into dashboard creation, ensure you have R and RStudio installed. You will also need to install the necessary packages:

```R
install.packages(c("flexdashboard", "plotly", "dplyr", "ggplot2"))
```

Once you have installed the packages, load them into your R session:

```R
library(flexdashboard) library(plotly) library(dplyr) library(ggplot2)
```

Creating the Flexdashboard Structure

Flexdashboard allows you to create dashboards using R Markdown. Start by creating a new R Markdown file:

In RStudio, click on **File > New File > R Markdown**.

Choose the **From Template** tab and select **Flex Dashboard**.

Name your document (e.g., `ai_dashboard.Rmd`), and click **OK**.

In the R Markdown file, you'll see a default template. Here's a basic skeleton you can use:

```markdown

---

title: "AI Dashboard" output:

flexdashboard::flex_dashboard: orientation: columns vertical_layout: fill

---

## Column {data-col=1}

### AI Model Performance

```{r}
# Code to generate performance plots will go here
```

```
```

You can add sections and customize the layout with headers, columns, and various visual components. ## Data Preparation

To illustrate the use of AI insights, let's simulate some data related to AI model performance. We can create a dataframe that holds the accuracy, precision, recall, and F1 score of different machine learning models:

```R
# Simulated AI Model Performance Data set.seed(123)
models <- c("Model A", "Model B", "Model C", "Model D")
```
```

```r
performance_metrics <- data.frame(
Model = models,
Accuracy = runif(4, 0.7, 1),
Precision = runif(4, 0.6, 1),
Recall = runif(4, 0.5, 1),
F1_Score = runif(4, 0.5, 1)
)
```

Creating Visualizations with plotly

Now that we have our data, we can create visualizations using **plotly**. We'll create an interactive bar plot to display the model performance metrics.

```R
### AI Model Performance
```{r}
# Interactive Bar Plot for Model Performance
performance_metrics_long <- performance_metrics %>%
gather(key = "Metric", value = "Value", -Model)

plot_performance <- plot_ly(performance_metrics_long,
x = ~Model, y = ~Value,
color = ~Metric, type = 'bar') %>%
layout(title = 'AI Model Performance Metrics', yaxis =
list(title = 'Score'),
barmode = 'group')
plot_performance
```
```

```
` ` `
```

Enhancing the Dashboard with Additional Features

To make your dashboard more informative, you can add further visualizations and interactivity. For instance, you can create separate plots for each performance metric or add filters that allow users to change visualizations based on certain criteria.

Adding a Line Plot for Model Comparisons

```R
```

Performance Comparison

```{r}
```

Line Plot for Visual Comparison of Metrics

plot_comparison <- ggplot(performance_metrics_long, aes(x = Model, y = Value, color = Metric)) + geom_line(aes(group = Metric), size = 1.2) +

geom_point(size = 3) +

labs(title = 'Model Performance Comparison', y = 'Score') +

theme_minimal()

ggplotly(plot_comparison)
```
` ` `
```

Adding Real-time Data

Incorporate real-time data to make your dashboards more dynamic. Using APIs or databases, you can fetch live model performance metrics and update them in your dashboard.

```R
# Example function to fetch data from an API (pseudo-code) fetch_real_time_data <- function(api_url) {

# Code to fetch and return data from the API

}
```

We have explored how to create dynamic and interactive AI dashboards using **flexdashboard** and

plotly within R. By combining the power of R's data manipulation and visualization capabilities, you can effectively communicate complex AI insights through intuitive dashboards.

As data continues to evolve, the way we present and interact with it must also advance. Leveraging tools like flexdashboard and plotly helps you stay at the forefront of data visualization, making AI's insights accessible to a broader audience.

Feel free to experiment with additional visualizations and enhancements, such as embedding maps, adding filters, or integrating user input for a more tailored experience. The possibilities are endless, limited only by your creativity and the needs of your audience.

Conclusion

In the rapidly evolving landscape of artificial intelligence (AI), the ability to harness data effectively is more crucial than ever. As organizations increasingly rely on data-driven strategies to inform their decisions, the need for professionals proficient in data analysis, modeling, and AI development has skyrocketed. Enter R, a powerful programming language that has emerged as one of the premier tools for statistical computing and data visualization in the realm of AI.

Welcome to "R Language for AI: Learn to Build Intelligent Models, Analyze Data, and Unlock AI's Full Potential Using R's Cutting-Edge Tools and Libraries." This book serves as a comprehensive guide for anyone looking to dive into the world of AI with R. Whether you're a complete beginner, a seasoned data scientist, or a professional seeking to expand your skill set, this resource will empower you to navigate the intricacies of AI development using R's innovative tools and libraries.

Throughout this book, we will explore the foundational concepts of R, demonstrate how to manipulate and analyze data efficiently, and guide you in building intelligent models that can drive insights and predictions. With a blend of theoretical knowledge and practical hands-on examples, you will learn to unlock the full potential of AI, applying its principles to real-world challenges across various industries.

You will discover how to leverage R's extensive ecosystem of libraries, such as `tidyverse` for data manipulation, `caret` for machine learning, and `keras` for deep learning, among others. Each chapter is designed to build on the last, ensuring a logical progression that reinforces your understanding while also challenging your capabilities. By the end of this journey, you will be equipped not only to use R for AI but also to think critically about what AI can achieve in your field of interest.

As we embark on this exploration of R and its role in AI, prepare to engage with the fascinating world of data science and machine learning. You will learn not just how to write code, but also how to interpret results, derive actionable insights, and frame questions that lead to meaningful outcomes. The world of AI is not just about algorithms and data—it's about storytelling, problem-solving, and making an impact.

Let's get started on this exciting journey to unlock the potential of R for AI and transform your data into knowledge!

Biography

Peter Simon is a passionate data scientist, educator, and lifelong learner who lives at the intersection of code and curiosity. With a deep-rooted expertise in **R programming**, **machine learning**, **bioinformatics**, and **artificial intelligence**, Peter has dedicated his career to making complex AI technologies accessible and practical for real-world use.

Peter holds a strong academic background in computational biology and has spent years applying AI and R-based solutions to challenges in healthcare, genetics, and data analytics. His unique ability to translate advanced concepts into clear, actionable steps has made him a trusted mentor for students, researchers, and professionals looking to dive into the world of intelligent systems.

When he's not crafting models or decoding data, Peter enjoys experimenting with open-source tools, contributing to the R community, and hiking through nature trails with a notebook full of ideas. He believes learning should be hands-on, fun, and a little bit messy— just like life itself.

"If you can teach a machine to think, you can teach yourself to think better." That's the philosophy Peter brings to every page of his work.

Glossary: R Language for AI

A

Algorithm

A step-by-step procedure or formula for solving a problem. In the context of AI and machine learning, algorithms are employed to learn from data and make predictions.

Analytics

The discovery and communication of meaningful patterns within data. In AI, analytics encompasses statistical analysis as well as advanced techniques like machine learning and deep learning.

B

Big Data

Extremely large datasets that may be analyzed computationally. R provides packages and tools for managing and analyzing big data effectively.

Bias

A systematic error that may occur in the data collection process or in the algorithmic approach, leading to incorrect predictions or interpretations.

C

Classification

A supervised learning technique used to predict categorical labels. R offers several packages such as `caret` and `randomForest` to facilitate classification tasks.

Clustering

An unsupervised learning technique that groups similar data points into clusters. Common algorithms used in R for clustering include k-means and hierarchical clustering.

Code

A set of instructions written in a programming language (in this case, R) that tells the computer how to perform a specific task.

D

Data Frame

A two-dimensional, table-like structure in R that can store data of different types. Data frames are commonly used to manipulate datasets in R.

Deep Learning

A subset of machine learning that involves neural networks with many layers. R provides packages like

`keras` and `tensorflow` to help implement deep learning models. ## E

Empirical Analysis

The process of gaining knowledge through direct and indirect observation or experience, particularly in statistics and data analysis.

Ensemble Methods

Techniques that combine multiple models to improve predictive performance. Common ensemble methods in R include bagging, boosting, and stacking.

F

Feature Engineering

The process of creating new features or selecting important features from raw data to improve the performance of machine learning models.

Function

A block of code in R that performs a specific task and can be reused multiple times throughout an analysis. ## G

Gradient Descent

An optimization algorithm used to minimize the loss function in machine learning models by iteratively adjusting parameters.

GPU (Graphics Processing Unit)

A hardware device designed to accelerate computations, particularly those involving large datasets or complex models. GPUs can significantly speed up model training in AI.

H

Hyperparameter

An external configuration variable in a machine learning model that determines the behavior of the training process. Common hyperparameters may include the learning rate, number of trees, or number of layers in a neural network.

I

Imputation

The process of replacing missing data with substituted values. R provides various methods for imputation through packages like `mice` and `missForest`.

J

JSON (JavaScript Object Notation)

A lightweight data interchange format that is easy for humans to read and write and easy for machines to parse and generate. R can handle JSON data using the `jsonlite` package.

K

K-Fold Cross-Validation

A technique used to assess the performance of machine learning models by partitioning the dataset into K subsets and training the model K times, each time holding out a different subset for validation.

L

Linear Regression

A statistical method for modeling the relationship between a dependent variable and one or more independent variables. R offers functions like `lm()` to perform linear regression.

Logistic Regression

A statistical method used for binary classification tasks, predicting the probability of the presence of a characteristic. The `glm()` function in R can be used for logistic regression analysis.

M

Metadata

Data that provides information about other data. In the context of R, metadata can include details about data structure, types, and source.

Model Evaluation

The process of assessing how well a machine learning model performs on a dataset. Common metrics used for evaluation in R include accuracy, precision, recall, and F1 score.

N

Neural Network

A computing system inspired by the human brain's networks of neurons. R facilitates neural network modeling through packages like `nnet` and `caret`.

O

Object

In R, an object is a data structure that can be manipulated using methods and functions. Everything in R—like vectors, lists, and data frames—is considered an object.

Overfitting

A modeling mistake where a model learns not only the underlying patterns in the training data but also the noise, leading to poor performance on unseen data.

P

PCA (Principal Component Analysis)

A dimensionality reduction technique that transforms data into a new coordinate system, highlighting the directions (principal components) of maximum variance. R has built-in functions and packages, like

`prcomp()`, to conduct PCA.

Predictive Modeling

The process of using statistical algorithms and machine learning techniques to identify the likelihood of future outcomes based on historical data.

Q

Quantile

A statistical term referring to dividing a dataset into equal-sized intervals. Quantiles include medians (50th percentile) and quartiles (25th and 75th percentiles), among others.

R

Regression

A technique for modeling the relationship between a dependent variable and one or more independent variables to make predictions.

RMarkdown

A file format that allows users to create dynamic documents, reports, and presentations that include R code and its output.

S

Sampling

The process of selecting a subset of individuals, items, or observations from a larger population to draw conclusions about that population. Techniques include random sampling and stratified sampling.

Supervised Learning

A type of machine learning where the model is trained on labeled data, meaning that the input comes with the correct output.

T

Tokenization

The process of breaking down text into smaller units, such as words or phrases, often used in natural language processing tasks.

Tuning

The process of adjusting hyperparameters in a model to optimize its performance. Common techniques include grid search and random search.

U

Unsupervised Learning

A type of machine learning where the model is trained on data without labeled responses. It focuses on analyzing the underlying structure of the data.

V

Variable

A characteristic or attribute that can vary across observations in a dataset. In R, variables are fundamental components of data analysis.

Visualization

The representation of data in graphical formats to identify patterns or insights. R excels at data visualization using packages like `ggplot2` and `lattice`.

W

Workflow

A sequence of processes or steps undertaken to complete a data analysis project, from data collection and cleaning to analysis and reporting.

X

XOR (Exclusive OR)

A logical operation that outputs true only when the inputs differ. XOR is often used in machine learning to illustrate concepts of data separation.

Y

Yield

In the context of machine learning or data analysis, yield refers to the output or results produced from a particular model or analytical approach.

Z

Z-score

A statistical measurement that describes a value's relationship to the mean of a group of values. It is used to identify how many standard deviations an element is from the mean.

www.ingramcontent.com/pod-product-compliance
Lightning Source LLC
Chambersburg PA
CBHW070947050326
40689CB00014B/3375